Leadership Selection and Appointment in China

Chen Zhong, Zhao Shiming, et al., Eds

Published by
ACA Publishing Ltd.
University House
11-13 Lower Grosvenor Place
London SW1W 0EX, UK
Tel: +44 (0)20 7834 7676 Fax: +44 (0)20 7973 0076
E-mail: info@alaincharlesasia.com

Web: www.alaincharlesasia.com
Beijing Office
Tel: +86(0)10 8472 1250 Fax: +86(0)10 5885 0639
Written by Wang Jinding, He Lisheng, Zhao Quanmin
Edited by David Lammie
Translated by Zhou Min
© People's Publishing House, 2015
This translation is published by ACA Publishing Ltd in association with People's Publishing House

ALL RIGHTS RESERVED. NO PART OF THIS
PUBLICATION MAY BE REPRODUCED IN MATERIAL FORM,
BY ANY MEANS, WHETHER GRAPHIC,
ELECTRONIC, MECHANICAL OR OTHER, INCLUDING
PHOTOCOPYING OR INFORMATION STORAGE, IN
WHOLE OR IN PART, AND MAY NOT BE USED TO PREPARE
OTHER PUBLICATIONS WITHOUT WRITTEN
PERMISSION FROM THE PUBLISHER.

The greatest care has been taken to ensure accuracy but the publisher can accept no responsibility for errors or omissions, or for any liability occasioned by relying on its content.
ISBN 978-1-910760-19-2
Leadership Selection and Appointment in China is available from the National Bibliographic Service of the British Library.

Preface

What is the state system of China? How has the Communist Party of China (CPC) managed to exercize long-term governance and to lead the Chinese people from one victory to another? What are the 'secrets' of the CPC's governance? What is China's development road? What significant strategies have been adopted in China? What is the next step in China's development? Why has China been able to achieve such rapid economic development? These are just some of the many questions frequently asked by the international community, especially foreign political parties and statesmen on their visits to China. For the purpose of providing answers to these questions and enabling readers to be informed about the real China and the CPC, we arranged for the *Understanding Modern China* Series (hereinafter referred to as the Series) to be written, to serve as elementary documents introducing the CPC, as well as China's development road, development theories and development experience.

The Series is inspired by the new philosophies, new ideas and new strategies for the country's governance put forward by General Secretary Xi Jinping since the 18th National Congress of the CPC, aimed at the following aspects: strenuously reflecting the development vision of 'the Chinese Dream' and the development prospects of the 'Two Centenary' goals; strenuously reflecting the coordinated promotion of the overall situation of a 'five-pronged approach to building socialism with Chinese characteristics to build up socialist economy, socialist democracy, socialist advanced culture, socialist harmonious society and socialist ecological civilisation; and the strategic arrangements for the 'Four-Pronged Comprehensive Strategy' comprehensively completing the building of a moderately prosperous society in all respects, comprehensively deepening reform in all respects, comprehensively advancing the rule of law, and comprehensively exercising strict discipline for the party; strenuously reflecting the 'new normal' facilitating and leading China's economic development and the implementation of the 'five major development concepts' to promote innovative, coordinated, green, open and shared development; strenuously reflecting the three major economic development strategies of the 'Belt and Road', the coordinated development of Beijing, Tianjin and Hebei province, and the Yangtze river economic belt. On the basis of a great number of fresh cases and experiences, the Series tells China's story, transmits China's voice, analyzes China's problems, and offers China solutions.

The Series has been written on the basis of telling China's story and transmitting China's voice, oriented around the following four aspects: the first is to illustrate the new measures taken to deepen reform since the 18th National Congress of the CPC, the new ideas on economic development and the new philosophy on foreign affairs, on the basis of an all-round introduction to the achievements since the reform and opening up; the second is to analyze the reason for the achievements, the underlying operating law, and the process of evolution, while presenting the development achievements of China's economy and society; the third is to keep to problem orientation and demand orientation, rather than attempt to be all-embracing and systematic, so as to clear up targeted doubts and confusion on the basis of the demands of foreign readers; the fourth is to introduce China not only in terms of 'where it is coming from', but also in terms of 'where it is going', for the purpose of enabling readers to know about China's historical development process on the one hand, and on the other hand, exemplifying and clarifying how China assures the organic unification of its past, present and future, the organic combination of legacy and innovation, and how China is planning its future development.

Under the guidance of the International Department of the CPC Central Committee, the writing of the Series has been organized by China Executive Leadership Academy Pudong (CELAP).

The International Department of the CPC Central Committee is the functional department of the CPC in charge of foreign affairs. So far, the CPC has established connections of various types with more than 600 political parties and organizations in over 160 countries and regions, which include left-wing and right-wing parties; both ruling parties and opposition parties. Foreign affairs work is of paramount importance to the CPC, and an indispensable component of national diplomacy as a whole, whose target is to promote state-to-state and people-to-people communication and understanding.

Preface

CELAP is a national leadership institution in China, and as a platform on which international cooperative training and exchange are carried out, CELAP has held fast to its characteristics of internationality and openness since March 2005 when it was founded. CELAP spares no effort in implementing international cooperative training, with target participants being foreign political parties and statesmen, high-ranking business executives and senior professionals. By the end of 2015, CELAP had offered training programs to more than 6,000 participants from over 130 countries, and thus has won wide recognition and received a favorable reception from the countries, regions and participants that are involved.

To cater for the needs of foreign participants, CELAP initiated the writing of the Series at the beginning of 2012, and after four years of modifications and improvements, the finalized manuscripts were completed at the end of 2015. The first batch of 10 books to be published in this Series are: *China's New Strategies for Governing the Country*; *The Communist Party of China: the Past, Present and Future of Party Building*; *China's Reform, Opening Up and Construction of Development Zones*; *The Framework of the Chinese Government and Public Services*; *A New Analysis of Urbanization in China*; *China's Agriculture and Rural Development in the Post-Reform Era*; *The Evolution of China's Diplomacy in the Modern Era*; *Leadership Selection and Appointment in China*; *Leadership Education and Training in China*; and *Shanghai – the 'Pacesetter' of China's Reform and Opening Up*.

The authors of the Series are mainly professionals in CELAP, and functionaries and specialists in the Development Research Center of the Shanghai Municipal People's Government, Shanghai Institute for International Studies and Hangzhou Research Center for Urban Studies.

The Series is published in Chinese and English, with the English translation done mainly by senior professors at Shanghai International Studies University, to whom thanks are due. Gratitude also goes to the People's Publishing House for its great support and positive suggestions in the process of writing and translating.

Writing such a series of textbooks for mature foreign students is a first in China. Constructive criticism is welcome, for the Series as a new endeavor can hardly be free from mistakes.

Editorial Committee of the *Understanding Modern China* Series
January 2016

The Editorial Committee of the Understanding Modern China Series

Directors: Guo Yezhou Feng Jun

Vice Directors: Zhou Zhongfei   An Yuejun

Members: (Listed alphabetically)

An Yuejun	Chen Zhong	Feng Jun
Guo Yezhou	He Lisheng	Jiang Haishan
Li Man	Li Yanhui	Liu Genfa
Liu Jingbei	Wang Guoping	Wang Jinding
Yang Jiemian	Zhao Shiming	Zheng Jinzhou
Zhou Zhenhua	Zhou Zhongfei	

Editor-in-Chief: Feng Jun

Alain Charles Asia (ACA) Publishing Ltd is delighted to be associated with the People's Publishing House to bring this series of 10 *Understanding Modern China* books to an English-speaking readership.

ACA, formerly known as ACP (Alain Charles Publishing) Ltd Beijing, was founded in October 1989 and was the first foreign-owned publishing company to be allowed to open an office in China.

In 2007, ACP Beijing was renamed ACA Publishing Ltd to better reflect its focus on China and the Asia-Pacific region. The company specialises in publishing books about China for international readers and has offices in Beijing and London.

ACA Publishing Ltd,

April 2016

Contents

Introduction X

Chapter 1   The Past and Present of the Selection and Appointment of Cadres in China 1

    1   The bureaucratic tradition of 'selection according to merit' in ancient China 1

    2   The development and reform of the selection and appointment of cadres in China 4

    3   The characteristics and experience of the selection and appointment of cadres in China 10

Chapter 2   The Basic System and Principal Methods of Selecting and Appointing Cadres 16

    1   The selection standard of cadres 16

    2   The requirements and qualifications of cadres 18

    3   The basic system of selecting and appointing cadres 21

    4   Major ways of selecting and appointing cadres 30

Chapter 3   The Working Principle of the Selection and Appointment of Cadres 32

    1   Cadres under the leadership of the CPC 32

    2   Selection according to merit from all corners of the country 34

    3   Selection according to morality and talent with morality before talent 37

    4   Selection according to achievements and public recognition 39

    5   Democratic, open, competitive and preferential selection .. 40

    6   Democratic centralism 42

    7   Principle of acting by law 43

Chapter 4	Compulsory Procedures of the Selection and Appointment of Cadres	47
1	Motion	48
2	Democratic recommendation	50
3	Investigation	52
4	Decision through discussion	58
5	Appointment	63
Chapter 5	Strict Administration of the Selection and Appointment of the Cadres	67
1	Strict selection before appointment	67
2	Strict check upon appointment	76
3	Strict management after appointment	79
Chapter 6	Examination and Evaluation in the Selection and Appointment of Cadres	88
1	Admission by exam for new civil servants	88
2	Public selection for civil servants in office	104
3	Competition and public selection for leadership posts	108
Chapter 7	Assessment and Examination in the Selection and Appointment of Cadres	114
1	Targeted assessment of the morality of cadres	114
2	Annual examination of cadres	122
3	Comprehensive evaluation and assessment	127
4	Usual assessment of cadres	135
Chapter 8	Discipline and Supervision of the Selection and Appointment of Cadres	137
1	Discipline	137
2	Supervision on selection and appointment	143
3	Accountability	158
Chapter Follow-up Questions and References		161

Introduction

The term 'cadre' has a wide range of meaning in China. Broadly speaking, it refers to every civil servant working for the country, including all those who work for the party in power, the government, People's Congress, Political Consultative Conference, as well as some public communities. More narrowly, cadres refer to officials who hold some office or enjoy some rank in the party or government; for example, 'leaders' and 'cadres' often refer to civil servants above the level of departmental leaders who work for the party and government.

The selection and appointment of cadres have played significant and fundamental roles in promoting the reform and opening-up process as well as economic and social development. Cadres constitute an elite group in Chinese society because they make up a huge number of top talents with idealism and wisdom; more important, these leaders have carried out the most significant work in the Chinese revolution and social construction and have become the pillar of the whole society. Since the Chinese Communist Party (CPC) was founded in 1921, the selection and appointment of cadres have been a central job in the party. Chairman Mao once said: "After we decide on the correct route, the role of cadres will become a decisive factor." ('The Status of Chinese Communist Party in the National War' in *Selected Writings of Mao Zedong*, Volume II). The selection and appointment of cadres paved the way for the victory of the Chinese revolution, the construction of the country and reform and opening up, with strong personnel and organization support.

The selection and appointment of cadres in China is a policy-based and scientific practice. The imperial examination system in the Sui and Tang dynasties was the earliest recognized cadre selection system, and it deeply influenced the system of civil servants in the UK and some other western countries. Since the establishment of the New China, the selection and appointment of cadres have undergone many developments and changes and have been transformed from a single assignment system to more scientific and effective multiple systems that include selection, assignment, examination and appointment. A series of systems and regulations has been designed so as to provide the selection system with enough policy support; at the same time, the method, technique and procedure of selection have become more democratic, open, competitive and preferential. New techniques in personnel selection and assessment have also been adopted, leading to an obvious improvement in the scientific level of the selection and appointment system of cadres.

First, attention is paid to the morality and talent of cadres, as well as the actual achievement in the selection and appointment. It takes many years of practice and experience, as well as strong idealism, noble character and outstanding leadership and professionalism for a newly appointed civil servant to grow into a higher leader for the party or government. Requirements such as experience, morality and professionalism demonstrate in the modern theory of cadre selection the importance of specific abilities for the targeted post. For the selection of leaders of the party and the government, selection based on competence rather than a single vote is more effective. Since there is a specific requirement for the experience, morality and professionalism of the appointed cadres in the selection system, it enables cadres who have been selected to fit into the new post better and faster, and to make more obvious achievements. In fact, in the personnel selection for the government in developed countries, selection according to competency is common practice. The idea and practice of the selection and appointment of cadres in China is comparatively advanced and practical. Selection based on morality, talent and achievement ensures that most selected leaders are competent for their posts, which increases the efficiency and quality of selection and appointment.

Second, selection and appointment of cadres in China is carried out in a democratic spirit and procedure. Ordinary party members and cadres are given sufficient information about the selection and appointment of cadres, and are involved in the supervision and selection process. Thanks to a transparent system, even common citizens are not unfamiliar with the procedure. Inside the party and the government, many democratic procedures are involved in promoting a cadre. For example, the selection of almost all cadres must go through a process of democratic recommendation; a sufficient number or proportion of people must approve the experience, morality and ability of the candidate before he or she can be promoted, otherwise no following procedures can be carried out. After the initial selection, the organizing and personnel department should try to listen to the opinion of different departments and colleagues and find the potential shortcomings of the candidate. After this, there will be a democratic assessment of the candidate. This procedure is called 'examination' in the selection process. Also, before formal appointment, there must be a public notification of people from a certain range of departments and party organizations. If there is a disagreement or problem with incompetence or a violation of discipline regarding the candidate to be promoted, ordinary party members or cadres can complain to the department in charge of selection or party committees and discipline inspection committees at a higher level. Such democratic procedures in selection and appointment ensures that most appointed leaders are approved of by the public.

Third, the selection and appointment of cadres follow the principle of leadership under the party as well as rule by category, which is a system that suits the national and political reality of China. Leadership under the party means that it is the party that administers and supervises cadres at different levels. The CPC is the party in power in China, and the power of administration of cadres is the highest power. Insistence on the party's control of cadres enable it to choose more effectively those who are faithful and committed to the tenet of the party, those who have high morals and high standards of behavior, and those who have the ability to make outstanding contributions to the country and society. Meanwhile, leadership of the party over cadres enables effective training, education and supervision of cadres so as to improve the efficiency of the management of cadres. The great achievement of China's reform and opening up is closely related to the fact that cadres are under the leadership of the party. While adhering to the leadership of the party in the administration of cadres, the selection and appointment of cadres in China conforms with the relative principles in personnel management. While following the principle of the party's direct leadership over important leaders in different fields and at different levels, a system of hierarchal and classified management is put into practice, in which the party and the government is separated, the government and the enterprise is separated, and at the same time, the management of business and the management of people are both closely related to each other and constrained by the other. Apart from selecting a large number of outstanding cadres inside the party, many excellent talents are also absorbed into the team of cadres for the national government, which promotes economic development, political stability and social progress of the country. The system, theory and practice of the selection and appointment of cadres, therefore, constitutes an important element of the different aspects of 'socialism with Chinese characteristics'.

Fourth, the selection and appointment of cadres in China is made under a strict process of management and supervision. Party organizations at different levels are in charge of the central management of selection and appointment. It is also emphasized that party organizations should check the process. The CPC has established the world's strictest procedure of management and supervision in the selection and appointment of cadres. For example, when someone is to be promoted to be a leader in the party or government organization (usually at the level of county government or department and above), his personal profiles must be checked, the authenticity of the report of his personal information (similar to the property declarations of public officials in the west) must be approved, the investigation of any disciplinary breaches of the party must be carried out by the department of discipline and supervision, and any report on breaches of party discipline must be addressed. Failure of such procedures will lead to the postponement or cancellation of the selection and appointment process. In addition, all appointed cadres must pass a one-year probation period. After one year, there will be a very strict investigation and assessment process. The organization department of the party has listed requirements concerning the actual process of selection and appointment, according to which, those who are 'selected in spite of sickness' will need to be assessed in terms of the selection process. If problems or flaws are discovered, both the organization and the individual will be put under investigation and held responsible. Such strict measures inside the party not only ensure the effective supervision of the selection and appointment process, but also ensure the party's powerful supervision of its organizations at different levels as well as the appointed leaders. These have played significant roles in maintaining quality and justice in the process of selection and appointment.

This book is a general introduction to the development of the selection and appointment of leaders in China, as well as the basic standards, the guiding principles and procedures, the measures concerning the strict management of selection and appointment, the technology used in exams and evaluation, the role of exams and evaluation in selection and appointment, and supervision, discipline and responsibility investigation. It will give readers a reasonably comprehensive and systematic knowledge of the procedures of selection and appointment of leaders in China.

This book was mainly written by Chen Zhong, Zhao Shiming and Ren Zhen, with contributions also from Wen Yanjuan and Yang Changyong.

Chapter 1

The Past and Present of the Selection and Appointment of Cadres in China

1 The bureaucratic tradition of 'selection according to merit' in ancient China

Governors in ancient China had long realized the importance of government administration and had established a relatively comprehensive system of selection, appointment and dismissal, examination and evaluation of administrators.[1]

Bureaucrats thought that 'the administrator is the basic foundation for the people';[2] if the administrator is righteous, the country can run smoothly. The administrators were encouraged to make 'governance of the state and peace on earth' their holy duty, and their commitment to the people and the country was accorded the highest value.

Considering the selection criteria, the morality of administrators was highly valued and a combination of morality and talent was emphasized. For example, Confucius once pointed out: "If a person has the talent and beauty of Master Zhou, yet he is proud and mean, the rest of the person is not worth considering."[3] With the relationship between morality and talent, Si Maguang contended that "talent is the supplement to morality, and morality is the guide for talent".[4] Although different standards of selection applied in different dynasties, some focusing on blood, some on military achievements, some on administrative ability, some on virtue and some on talent, the

---

[1] Research group of the Institute of the Party's Construction of the Ministry of Organization of the Central Committee of the CPC. *Research on the Reform and Expansion of the Chinese System of the Selection and Appointment of Leaders.* Beijing: Press of the Readings of the Construction of the Party, 2011, pp7-8
[2] According to Han Fei Zi, the administration of officials is the foundation of the governance of the people. A wise emperor would rule over officials rather than the common people govern the country
[3] See *Analytics Taibo*, even though someone is as talented as Master Zhou, he would not be appointed as an official if he is immoral, proud or mean
[4] See *History as a Mirror*, meaning talent is the supplement of virtue and virtue is the guide to talent

general trend was always towards a combination of virtue and talent, with virtue coming first.

In terms of selection and appointment, different ways of examination, appointment and evaluation have developed. For example, Han Feizi proposed that leaders should be evaluated according to the responsibilities of their positions.[5] "Judgment by position and evaluation by achievement to see whether the administrator lives up to the requirements of his post."[6] "Appointment is based on ability." In the Warring States period (475-221 BCE), leaders were put on probation. The imperial examination system is a typical example of 'selection by merit', which abolishes the boundaries of rich and poor, nobility and commoners, and adopts a principle of fair competition and selection according to merit.

With the evaluation of administrators, a very strict evaluation system was established to regularly check the performance of officials by means of interview, budget check, inspection etc. The measures used to assess officials include justice, implementation, prudency and integrity. Some different standards apply to different posts; those who fulfil their duties will be given credit while those who fail will be punished.

With regard to the administration of officials, strict and normative systems of avoidance and responsibility accountability were established: a local official can only hold office in places outside his own home region, central leaders should not hold office in Beijing, children of high officials should avoid inspection jobs, and relatives should not work in the same department. If the recommended applicant fails to carry out his responsibilities, the names of the family who recommend the applicant would be published, and in serious cases, nine generations of this family would be implicated.

Regarding the supervision of administrators, attention is paid to the balance between powers and duties. The supervision organization is relatively independent, and is under the direct leadership of superior departments. Officials in the department of supervision enjoy a high position and considerable power, which leads to a rather strict surveillance system.

---

[5] See *Hanfeizi*, meaning to evaluate an official according to his post and actual achievement
[6] See *Hanfeizi*, meaning to judge an official in his post, test him in experiment and evaluate him according to his actual achievements

Chapter 1

Column 1-1 The imperial examination system

The imperial examination system was a system to select officials through examination in feudal China. This system came into being in 605 in the first year of the reign of Da Ye, the second emperor of the Sui dynasty, was developed in the Tang dynasty, and matured gradually in the Song dynasty, Yuan dynasty and Ming dynasty. The system lasted about 1,300 years and was abolished in the 31st year of Emperor Guangxu in the Qing dynasty (1905).

The creativity of the imperial examination system is demonstrated in the following aspects: First, it symbolized the establishment of the standard of selecting leaders according to talent. This system abolished an aspect of the old reference system in which the opinion of higher officials played a decisive role, and kept the standard of knowledge of candidates within the old system. Its history of more than 1,000 years demonstrated its durability. Second, the imperial examination system represented the principle of fairness and equality in the selection of administrators. Under the common standard of knowledge, common people were provided with opportunities that were previously not open to them. "Peasant boy in the morning, court official in the afternoon."[7] According to a survey of about 900 jinshi (scholars who have passed the last grade in the imperial examination system and therefore can be offered a higher position), half of them came from the countryside in the Ming and Qing dynasties. Various measures were established by each dynasty to prevent and punish plagiarism, including the 'lock system' for the chief examiner, who is secluded from the outside world during the examination season. Also, in order to prevent corruption among privileged people, the parents of the examinee were not allowed to be examiners and if the children of officials took part in the exam, it was up to the emperor to make the final decision. Such strict restrictions on the privilege of the feudal bureaucratic class demonstrated the principle of fairness. Third, the imperial examination included education of talented students, selection by exam and evaluation.

These three elements helped establish a complete system of the education, selection and appointment of officials, which abided by the principle of

---

[7] See *The History of Pipa*, meaning that, in the morning one is still a country man, yet through hard work that enables him to pass the exam, in the evening he can be promoted to become a court official. The imperial examination system is a bridge between the lower and upper classes of society; passing the exam can elevate someone to the air from the dirt

fair competition and selection on the basis of merit. With this, abundant experiences and lessons were learned in term of both the theory and practice of the selection and appointment of officials. The modern system of selecting civil servants is derived from the imperial exams.

2 The development and reform of the selection and appointment of cadres in China

The selection and appointment of cadres is an issue that encompasses the reason for selection, how to select and how to deploy the candidate after selection. Since the foundation of the New China, constant efforts have been made evaluate the system of the selection and employment of cadres.

(1) The management, selection and appointment of cadres before 1953

Before 1953, the selection and appointment of cadres in China were under the unified and comprehensive management of the central government and the organization department of party committees. Before the founding of the New China, to suit the situation and meet the needs of war, all cadres were selected and appointed by party organizations. At the beginning of the New China, this system was inherited and adopted. Apart from military leaders, the selection and appointment of all local leaders were under the unified management of the central committee and the organization departments of the party. This highly centralized system of selecting and appointing cadres made it possible to select and deploy cadres effectively, strengthening the cadre team in important regions and departments, and ensuring the completion of works and tasks. At the same time, any disunity in the implementation of the party's cadre policy could be avoided or mitigated.

In order to meet the needs of war, the selection and appointment of cadres in this period mainly adopted the commission system, through which cadres were selected and promoted according to the practice of revolutionary struggles and that of mass work. The appointment of leaders of party organizations and local government also adopted the election system. In accordance with *The Constitution Outline of the Soviet Republic of China*, the systems for election, commission and selection were all adopted in cadre selection and promotion. The constitution passed at the second national congress of the CPC clearly stipulated that the chief leaders of party organizations at all levels were recommended among committee members who themselves were recommended and elected by party members. Moreover, the party's Central

Executive Committee was elected at party congress. It was stipulated in *The Third Amendment of the Constitution of the CPC* that the general secretary of the Central Committee should be elected.

(2) The management, selection and appointment of cadres from 1953 to 1978

With the founding of the New China, economic and social development became the focus of the work of the party and the state. Moreover, social labor division also demanded a classified management of cadres. In November 1953, the Central Committee of the CPC promulgated *Decision on Strengthening Cadre Management*, classifying the leading cadres into nine categories: army, culture and education, planning and industry, finance and trade, transportation, agriculture, forestry and water conservancy, democratic parties, politics and law, the party and the masses. With regard to hierarchical management, the aim was to establish a hierarchical system of cadre management in the Central Committee and party committees at all levels. Cadres holding important positions of state were selected and managed by the Central Committee while other cadres were selected and managed by party committees at corresponding levels. This system has played a positive role in the unification of the country's politics and economy and has also brought about socialist reform and large-scale economic construction.

Cadre selection and appointment in this period was still a highly unified commission system; it lacked innovation in system construction and appointment methods.

(3) The management, selection and appointment of cadres since 1978

After the implementation of the reform and opening-up policy in 1978, especially with the gradual establishment and development of China's socialist market economy, the cadre selection and appointment system was no longer applicable to the new circumstances. Therefore, the Central Committee of the CPC began to carry out substantial reform and innovation in the process. The reform of the cadre selection and appointment system passed through five important stages of development:

Phase one: 1978 to 1982

During this period, with the changes in the CPC's organizational line and cadre selection and appointment, the reform of the selection and appointment system of leading cadres emerged. Two of the most significant features of this reform were, first, the approach of a revolutionary, younger, knowledgeable, professional cadre team was proposed in order to adapt to the actual needs of economic reform and opening up; second, the existence of the system of life tenure in leading posts was abolished in order to promote a more vigorous system of cooperation and replacement of old cadres with new cadres. The four criteria of cadres (see Column 1-2) was the working principle of overall construction, which was significant in selecting and appointing cadres. Meanwhile, abolishing the system of life tenure in leading posts revolutionized the CPC'S cadre management policy, which institutionalized and standardized the replacement of old cadres with new ones by strictly enforcing the retirement system.

> **Column 1-2: The four criteria of cadres**
>
> *It was formally written into the party constitution at the 12th National Congress of the CPC that "a revolutionary, younger, more knowledgeable and professional cadre team should be realized" so as to resolve the contradiction between the structure and quality of the cadre team and the needs of reform and opening up. Raising the basic standards, 'the four criteria' was an important policy in the selection and appointment of cadres at the early stage of China's reform and opening up. To be revolutionary was to set up a correct world outlook, life outlook and values with a firm political belief and good moral character. To be young required cadres to be in the prime of life and energetic in order to be competent. To be knowledgeable required cadres to master adequate scientific and cultural knowledge. To be professional required cadres to have enough ability to become an expert in their work. The four criteria – to be revolutionary, young, knowledgeable and professional – was an organic whole, setting comprehensive standards for cadre selection and appointment.*

Phase two: 1983 to 1994

The 1983 National Organization Work Forum conducted a serious study into the management system of cadres. In October of the same year, the Central Organization Department issued *A Regulation on the Reform of the Management System of Cadres*, putting forward the principle of 'less control, flexible management and better administration' as well as classification management. This cadre reform was designed mainly to cater to the new requirements of economic system reform, in which the decentralization of management authority and classified management should be implemented.

In July 1984, the central government decided to decentralize and transfer to the lower level of the authority of cadre management and establish the system of 'one-rank management'. The Central Organization Department revised the job title of central management cadres and expanded the management authority of subordinate committees, SOEs and institutions, which mobilized the enthusiasm of cadres and cadre management institutions.

In 1987, the 13th Congress of the CPC put forward a new way to focus on the establishment of a civil servant system and implement the classified management of cadres. Thereafter the comprehensive reform of the cadre and personnel system of party committees, government agencies, SOEs and institutions was carried out. In 1992, the political bureau of the Central Committee passed the policy of *The Central Committee of the CPC's Views on Strengthening Party Construction and Improving Party Forces in Reform and Development*, stressing the need to adhere to the principle of cadres under the leadership of the CPC, and gradually establish and complete the classified management system, competition mechanism and mobilization mechanism in order to mobilize the enthusiasm of cadres and provide an institutional guarantee for outstanding talent to be promoted.

In August 1993, the State Council promulgated *Interim Regulations of National Civil Servants*, which was implemented on October 1 of the same year and tried out in the party, the NPC, the CPPCC and people's organizations. With the reform of the economic system, especially the deepening of the reform of SOEs, a big step was taken in the reform of the enterprise personnel management system. Cadres in enterprises and their corresponding administrative level were gradually decoupled, and the employment system of management personnel and professional and technical personnel of enterprises began to be carried out. The selection and appointment of leading personnel adopted approaches including commission, democratic election, public selection and open recruitment. The appointment system of professional and technical posts in public institutions was also introduced. To sum up, the main characteristics of the reform of cadre selection and appointment at this stage was to initially establish a classified management system of party committees, government agencies, enterprises and institutions.

Phase three: 1994 to 2014

In September 1994, the fourth plenary session of the 14th CPC Central

Committee passed *Decisions on Several Major Issues of Strengthening the Party's Construction by the Central Committee of the CPC*, accelerating the reform of the cadre selection and appointment system, in which 'democratic expansion, evaluation completion, exchange promotion and supervision reinforcement were stressed to ensure the gradual formation of the personnel mechanism of vigor and vitality', in which highly talented people would be given the chance to excel themselves. Thereafter, the reform of cadre selection, appointment and management has made great progress in many aspects.

In 1995, *The Interim Regulations on the Selection and Appointment of Leading Cadres of the Party and Government*, the party's first regulations on cadre selection and appointment, were promulgated and implemented. The principles, conditions, inspection methods and decision-making procedures of the selection and appointment of leading party and government cadres were clearly set out in the regulations, showing that China's cadre selection and appointment system was being standardized, institutionalized and legalized.

Through *Opinions on the Implementation of a Competition System for Party and Government Organizations*, issued by the Central Organization Department of the CPC Central Committee and the State Ministry of Personnel in 1998 and *Notice on Furthering the Public Selection of Leading Cadres* issued by the Central Organization Department in March 1999, appointment by way of competition and public selection were quickly accepted and applied nationwide. The main feature of cadre selection and appointment in this phase was to explore the modes of cadre selection and appointment. Many local and grassroots party organizations explored the specific ways and means of cadre selection and appointment reform, creating fresh experience of selection, publicity before appointment, competition for posts, competitive elections, recommendation appointments and other forms of reform.

In 2002, *Regulations on the Selection and Appointment of Leading Cadres of the Party and Government* further accelerated the pace of system reform of the selection and appointment of leading cadres, solidifying the achievements of former reform with state laws and party regulations. The following 12 cadre selection and appointment systems were formally implemented: the responsibility system of inspection, the pre-post publicity system, the probation system, the appointment system for some leadership positions, the exchange system of cadres, the 'avoidance' system of cadres, the 'avoidance' system of the work of cadre selection and appointment, the resignation system, the demotion system, the supervision system, the investigation system and the joint conference system of organization and personnel departments and discipline inspection organs (supervision department).

In 2003, the Central Organization Department issued *The National Examination Outline of the Public Selection of Leading Party and Government Cadres (Provisional)*, marking a new stage of the scientific and standardized examination system for public selection. The interview section introduced advanced personnel evaluation methods, such as a structured interview, culture tests and non-leading group discussions, in which the scientific element of evaluation was significantly enhanced. In short, the regulatory system of cadre selection, appointment and comprehensive management was basically formed in this phase.

Phase four: 2014 to the present

After the 18th National Congress of the CPC, while succeeding and fully affirming the reform measures in leading cadre selection and appointment, the Central Committee of the CPC modified some problems that appeared in system innovation. In January 2014, the revised *Regulations on the Selection and Appointment of Leading Party and Government Cadres* was formally promulgated and implemented, in which the principle of cadres under the leadership of the CPC were strengthened, and the leadership and powers of decision-making and supervision of party organizations (party committees and organization departments) in terms of cadre selection and appointment were stressed. At the same time, the Central Committee of the CPC also promulgated and implemented a series of strict management rules and regulations of cadre selection and appointment, which promoted cadre selection and appointment system construction to new heights through more stringent procedures on selection, supervision and responsibility accountability. The new regulations were a more perfect and mature concept and system of China's cadre selection and appointment.

Column 1-3 Cadres, party members as cadres, leading cadres, leading cadres of the party and government

Cadre is a foreign word that comes from the Latin word quodrum and later absorbed into English, French, Russian and Japanese. China's use of the word came from Russian transliteration during the period of revolution and war. At that time, cadres referred to members of the public who participated in revolutionary work and carried out certain responsibilities. After the PRC was founded, the word came to refer to anyone who was paid for by public funds, or members of party committees, state organs, democratic parties and people's organizations, or management staff and various professional and technical personnel of enterprises and institutions (non-governmental and public service institutions). National civil servants constitute the main body of cadres.

Leading cadres generally refer to those holding leadership positions in party committees, state bodies, democratic parties, people's organizations, SOEs and institutions. According to the party's working documents, leading cadres in the party and government refers to leading members above county (department) level who serve in party committees, the standing committee of the NPC, government agencies, CPPCC, the Disciplinary Committee of the party, the people's courts and People's Procuratorate. Leading members of departments of the above institutions are also classified as leading cadres.

3 The characteristics and experience of the selection and appointment of cadres in China

Viewing the selection of government and party cadres throughout the world, China's system and practice has distinct characteristics and advantages. To some extent, the unprecedented achievements of China's reform and opening up could be attributed to the reform and innovation of the system of selection and appointment of cadres. The selection and appointment of cadres has played an encouraging and guiding role, assembling a large number of outstanding talented individuals with the most abundant knowledge, ability and innovative spirit to the body of cadres.

(1) The major characteristics of the selection and appointment of cadres in China

Compared with the other parties and states, what are the distinctive characteristics of China's cadre selection and appointment? They are mainly demonstrated in the following aspects:[8]

---

[8] Dai Xiaoshu. 'The Basic Situation of the Selection and Evaluation System of Party and Government Leaders in China', *The Compilation of the Forum on the Selection and Training of Leaders of China and Singapore*, The Cadre Education Bureau of the CPC Central Committee, 2009, pp.47-48

1 The standard of selection: selection according to morality and talent with morality before talent

'Selection according to morality and talent with morality before talent' is a consistent principle of cadre selection and appointment by the CPC; it is also the crystalized representation and core content of the CPC's cadre line as well as the fundamental standard for selecting and appointing cadres. *Regulations on the Appointment of Cadres* adheres to the principle and standard of 'selection according to morality and talent with morality before talent' providing the basic conditions of leading cadres. The general requirement is that leading party and government cadres should be 'reliable in politics, professional in work ability, proficient in work style and trustworthy to the people', of which 'morality' and 'talent' are the two indispensable traits for cadres. Handling the relationship between morality and talent, we should always keep the former in foremost place. The morality of cadres mainly includes political morality, professional morality, family virtue and social morality. What is specially evaluated in cadre selection and appointment is whether cadres hold firm and ideal beliefs, whether they administrate for the people, whether they seek truth as well as handle concrete matters, and whether they adhere to democratic centralism. In other words, selected cadres should be honest, reliable and virtue-oriented. They should take responsibility, be diligent, practical, self-disciplined and down to earth, have a good reputation and place value on honesty.

2 Modes of selection: democracy and publicity, and common recognition of the people

Regulations on the Appointment of Cadres emphasized the need to further expand democracy in the work of cadres, implementing the people's right to know, to participate, to choose and to supervise cadre selection and appointment, with the goal of enhancing transparency in the task of selection and appointment. Currently, the selection and appointment of party and government leaders consists of six basic procedures: democratic recommendation, inspection, consideration, discussion and decision, lawful nomination and democratic consultation, and appointment. At the same time, the system based on these six procedures was established. Adhering to democratic recommendation as the basis of cadre selection and appointment, democratic evaluation, polls and extended inspections are actively implemented, enabling more people to participate in the process and thereby improving the quality of inspection. Meanwhile, the implementation of an inspection notice and publicity before appointment provides a smooth channel for informing the public and highlighting any problems. In this way, the opinion of the masses is widely heard. All these measures aim to select talented and able individuals who are well known to the public and who have political integrity and an outstanding track record to leading posts at various levels.

3 **The objects in selection: wide selection and fair competition**

For the cause of the party and the people, the vision of recognizing talent is expanded, the channel of selecting talent is broadened and the road of appointing talent is smoothed, all of which is designed to ensure a flexible selection and appointment process. Actively introducing the competition mechanism, we implemented public selection and competition for posts to promote competition and ensure the selection of outstanding cadres. Moreover, exploring the selection mechanism, we endeavor to improve the quality of the selection and appointment of cadres. Selecting talent is not only about the individual selection of leaders, it is also a democratic, public and competitive selection process that involves casting the net wide. Meanwhile, competitive nomination, recommendation, inspection and consideration are actively implemented, through which the responsibilities and requirements of the positions and the ability of cadres are comprehensively and comparatively analyzed. To expand democracy in the selection and appointment of cadres, the voting system of party committees for important posts and exploring competitive voting are generally pursued to enhance competition, improve voting quality and choose the most talented candidates.

4 **The management of selection: adherence to act by law and emphasis on supervision**

Our party has a strict supervision and inspection system for the selection and appointment of cadres. *Regulations on the Appointment of Cadres* stipulates that the task of selecting and appointing cadres must comply with the 10 disciplines ('The 10 Nos'), which plays an important role in ensuring the right selection and appropriate appointment in order to improve the quality of selection and appointment work. In practical work, we also endeavor to increase supervision and inspection, opening the '12380' reporting website and telephone hotlines, carrying out a satisfaction poll of the selection and appointment of cadre work, and strengthening the examination of all local and departmental implementation of *Regulations on the Appointment of*

Cadres. Informing the masses of the selection policies and standards, the necessary procedures and methods, and relevant feedback, we ensure the masses receive timely information and effective supervision of the work of cadre selection and appointment and the candidates in order to improve the credibility of the process.

(2) The major experience of the selection and appointment of cadres in China

In the 30 years of reform and opening up, from the abolition of the life tenure system in leading posts and the implementation of public selection, competition for posts, democratic recommendation, democratic appraisal, to the preliminary establishment of the regulations of cadre and personnel, China's reform of the cadre and personnel system, especially the work of selection and appointment, has made great achievements, which could be summarized as follows:[9]

- The principle of a revolutionary, younger, knowledgeable and professional cadre team has been clearly proposed and completely implemented so that the structure and overall quality of the cadre team has been significantly improved.
- The existence of the system of life tenure in leading posts has been abolished so that the replacement of old with new leading cadres has been institutionalized, standardized and made routine.
- Through the decentralization of the management authority and the implementation of cadre classification management, the establishment of a sound and scientific management system of cadres has made significant achievements.
- The reform measures to expand democracy have been widely implemented, so that the degree of democratization of the work of cadre selection and appointment has been improved.
- The cadre assessment work has been standardized and improved, which has played an important role in the selection of cadres.
- The practice of cadre exchange has been increased, and the exchange of leading cadres in important departments and key positions has been gradually developed into a system.

---

[9] Central Organization Department of the CPC. *The Course of Organization Work of the CPC*. Beijing: Party Construction Reading Press, 2006, pp. 299-300

- The cadre education and training system has been continuously improved, and the training system of cadre education with Chinese characteristics has begun to be formed.
- The supervision of cadres has been constantly strengthened, playing a positive role in curbing the phenomenon and tendency of corruption.
- The construction of a new system has made great strides, in which a coordinated, cohesive and complete set of work regulations of cadres and personnel has been initially formed.
- Through overall planning and procedures, the reform of the personnel system in SOEs and institutions has made additional progress and achievements.

Since reform and opening up, China's mode of cadre selection and appointment has been transformed from single to multiple, the procedure of cadre selection and appointment of cadres has been transformed from secretive to democratic, and the process of cadre selection and appointment has been transformed from self-discipline to supervision. The practice of the reform of cadre selection and appointment can be summarized as follows:[10]

- It is necessary to adhere to the correct direction of reform, to obey and serve the central task of the party and the state, and to make contributions to socialist economic construction, political construction, document construction, social construction as well as party building.
- System construction should be fundamental, building a cadre selection and appointment mechanism that conforms to China's national conditions, so that the scientific, standardized and legal system of selecting and appointing cadres is promoted.
- The expansion of democracy should be core, enhancing the openness and transparency of the work of cadres, and furthering the implementation of the people's right to understand, participate in, select and supervise selection and appointment work.

---

[10] Research Group of Party Building Research Institute of the Central Organization Department of the CPC Central Committee. *An Extended Research on the System Reform of Selecting and Appointing Cadres with Chinese Characteristics.* Beijing: Party Building Reading Press, 2011, p. 361

- It is necessary to be people-oriented, grasping the key links to find, train and use talented individuals so that the enthusiasm, initiative and creativity of cadres can be developed.
- Capacity building should be the focus, comprehensively improving the ability of cadres to perform their duties, to learn and innovate, so that the all-round development of cadres is promoted.

Chapter 2

The Basic System and Principal Methods of Selecting and Appointing Cadres

1 The selection standard of cadres

The selection standard is the basis and prerequisite for the selection and appointment of cadres. As the basic principles of cadre selection and appointment system and practice, 'selection according to morality and talent with morality before talent' is also the general standard of cadre selection and appointment. Therefore, in general, the selection standard of cadres is 'selection according to morality and talent with morality before talent'. At the sixth plenary session of the sixth Central Committee of the CPC held in October 1938, Mao Zedong held that "a combination of competence and integrity" and "appointment on merit" should be the standard in cadre selection and appointment. He went on: "The cadre policy of the Communist Party should be implementing party line, subjecting to party discipline, caring for the masses, being independent in work, and being motivated and unselfish."

Different stages of development and historical periods require a modification of focus on the standard of selection and appointment of cadres. Therefore, the selection standard of cadres is both specific and historical. In different historical periods, the specific requirements of cadres vary. In wartime, loyalty, bravery and sacrifice were considered the standard of cadre selection. However, during the socialist revolution and construction, cadres were supposed to be politically and professionally competent, that is, to be socialist-minded and professionally competitive. Moreover, in the early stage of China's reform and opening up, many young and educated cadres were urgently needed, and in this sense the basic standards of selection and appointment required cadres to be revolutionary, young, knowledgeable and professional. Entering the 21st century when China's reform and opening up was passing through a new development phase, the party raised a new adaptive standard that emphasized a combination of integrity and ability with integrity ahead of ability.

In 2013, at the national organization meeting, the general secretary of the CPC Central Committee, comrade Xi Jinping, clearly put forward the standard of good cadres as being "strong in belief, enthusiastic at serving the people, diligent and pragmatic, responsible and accountable, and upright and honest", bringing new elements to the process of cadre selection. General Secretary Xi also pointed out at the meeting: "Cadre standards, in a broader sense, are a combination of integrity and ability. To sum up, good cadres should be enthusiastic in serving the people, diligent and pragmatic, responsible and accountable, and upright and honest."

- To be strong in belief means all selected cadres should be sincere believers of Marxism, communism and socialism. They should recognize, adhere to and defend, in all circumstances, the party's basic theory, basic line, basic program, basic experience and basic requirements. Holding firm political beliefs is the most important standard of cadre selection, which is the core of cadres' 'integrity'.

- To be enthusiastic in serving the people requires loyalty to the people. Selected cadres should perform as servants of the people, with their joys and sorrows shared with the people. They should connect with the people, serve the people, do all things for the people and depend on the people. They should come from the masses and go to the masses. The purpose of the CPC is to serve the people, besides which no interests of the party exist. Serving the people with heart and soul is the basic responsibility of party cadres, and it is also an important standard of cadre selection.

- To be diligent and pragmatic requires selected leaders to be dedicated to their work. They should be able to seek truth as well as handle concrete matters, endeavor to work hard and in a practical manner, and constantly strive for perfection. On performing specific duties, party cadres must work conscientiously, act in accordance with objective law, seeking truth from facts, and conscientiously perform their duties, so as to make achievements that can stand the test of the people and history. Diligence and implementation are important requirements of the working style of cadres.

- To be responsible and accountable refers to the adherence to principle, fulfillment in duty and courage to shoulder responsibility. Considering the diversity of modern society and the new stage of China's reform and opening up, selected party cadres need to be brave enough to adhere to their political stance ahead of the major issues of principle. In times of difficulty, selected cadres should dare to stand up and be counted. In addition, addressing mistakes that have been made, they should dare to take responsibility, giving no excuses and showing no evasion.

– Being upright and honest requires selected cadres to be clear about differentiating between public and private matters. They should reject corruption and be thrifty. They should endure hardship, correctly exercise their public power, and hold their political and moral integrity so as to be honest in governance, in the use of power, in self cultivation and in personal household management. Honesty is the moral standard for cadres and integrity is essential.

China's economic and social development has entered a new historical period. The five standards of good cadres are the latest requirements of the CPC Central Committee on the selection and appointment of cadres. On different occasions, General Secretary Xi Jinping has made specific requirements of cadre standards in different fields and departments. As to the party's grassroots leadership, namely secretaries of county party committees, General Secretary Xi put forward the 'four haves' standard: to be loyal to the party, committed to the people, responsible in heart and disciplined in mind. These are also highly consistent with the five standards of good cadres.

In October 2014, on an inspecting tour to Yunnan province, General Secretary Xi made important instructions, requiring party members and cadres "to be loyal to the party, to be clean-handed as individuals, to be brave in shouldering responsibility". This concise description summarized the standards expected of good cadres. Loyalty is the political character of party cadres, and personal probity is essential and bravery to shoulder responsibility is the professional quality.

2 The requirements and qualifications of cadres

'The Ordinance on Cadre Selection and Appointment' clearly defines the requirements of leading cadres, embodying the CPC's basic requirements of leading cadres at all levels in terms of ideological and political quality, organization and leadership ability, ideological and work style.

(1) The requirements of cadres

In accordance with 'The Ordinance on Carder Selection and Appointment', the six basic requirements of leading cadres are as follows:

- Leading cadres should consciously adhere to Marxism and Leninism, Mao Zedong thought, Deng Xiaoping theory, the 'Three Represents' and the 'Scientific Outlook on Development'. Analyzing and solving practical problems from a Marxist viewpoint and approach, leading cadres should keep learning, understand politics, stress moral rectitude, and be highly consistent with the Central Committee in ideology, politics and action so as to withstand all kinds of trials and tribulations.

- Leading cadres should possess a lofty ideal of communism and a firm faith in socialism with Chinese characteristics. Besides, they should firmly implement the party's basic lines, principles and policies, commit to reform and opening up, and dedicate to the cause of modernization. Moreover, they should pioneer arduously in socialist construction and establish correct achievement view, making achievements that can stand the tests of practice, people and history.

- Leading cadres should emancipate the mind, seek truth from facts and keep pace with the times. They should be true, practical and serious with regard to investigation and research, so that they can combine party principles and policies with the reality of specific areas and departments to ensure fruitful work. They should also tell the truth, do practical things, seek practical results and oppose formalism.

- Leading cadres should have a strong sense of revolutionary commitment, political responsibility, practical experience, and the qualified organizational skills, education and professional knowledge needed by the organization.

- Leading cadres should rightly exercise the power entrusted by the people. They should adhere to the principles, dare to administrate, act in accordance with the law, remain honest and work diligently for the people. They should also make themselves an example of hard work and plain living, diligence and thrift. They should form close ties with the masses, adhere to the mass party line, and consciously accept the criticism and supervision from both the party and the masses. They should emphasize moral cultivation and party spirit, integrity and exemplary conduct. To take the lead in practicing socialist core values, cadres should actively make themselves respectable, introspective, alert and encouraging, opposing bureaucracy, the abuse of power and the illegitimate desire for profit.

– Leading cadres should stand for democratic centralism of the party, exhibiting a democratic style of work and taking a holistic view. They should unite comrades, including those who have different work views.

(2) The qualifications of cadres

'The Ordinance on Cadre Selection and Appointment' also clearly defines the specific qualifications in selecting and appointing cadres, which includes work length and experience, work tenure, educational background, continued training and any necessary physical conditions for specific positions.

– The promotion of county-level leadership and middle-rank leadership shall be open to those with at least five years' work experience and a grassroots working experience of two years.

– The promotion of leadership at or above county or department levels should usually satisfy a work experience of at least two positions of a lower rank.

– As for promotions at or above county or department levels, applicants from deputies wanting to become chiefs should have worked for more than two years in the deputy position; and if promoted from the lower chief position to the higher deputy position, cadres should have work in the lower chief position for more than three years. The tenure of the promotion of high-rank non-leadership positions is implemented in accordance with the relevant requirements.

– Most promoted cadres should have a junior college education, and promoted cadres at bureau level should have received a university education, at least.

– Promoted cadres should have received training from a party school, administrative college, cadre college or another training institution recognized by the organization or personnel department. The training period should also meet the relevant requirements of cadre education and training. Those cadres who fail to meet the requirements of training but have a reasonable excuse should receive training within one year of promotion.

- Promoted cadres should be in good physical condition necessary for the post.
- The promotion of cadres should comply with the requirements of the relevant laws and regulations. The promotion of the party leadership should also comply with the provisions of *The Constitution of the CPC* in terms of how many years they have been a party member.

'The Ordinance on Cadre Selection and Appointment' also stipulates that outstanding cadres or cadres who are in special demand can break through the appointment qualifications or be promoted to a more senior leadership, otherwise known as 'exceptional promotion' and 'above-rank promotion'. However, 'The Ordinance on Cadre Selection and Appointment' also sets out rigorous regulations for such circumstances. For example, outstanding cadres who deserve exceptional promotion should be prominent both in morality and ability; should be highly recognized by the masses; and should meet one of the following requirements. First, he should accomplish difficult tasks, perform outstandingly and make a significant contribution at a crucial moment or have endured a difficult and perilous task. Second, he should have already made prominent achievements in areas or departments that are difficult, complex and poor. Third, he should be conscientious and responsible in other posts and have made particularly significant achievements. Furthermore, the exceptional promotion of cadres must be strictly controlled. Under no circumstance should cadres be promoted beyond the required conditions and qualifications. In addition, cadres who are still within a probationary period who have been promoted within the past year should not be promoted exceptionally. Moreover, cadres should not enjoy exceptional promotion continuously in his tenure, and they should not be promoted beyond two ranks.

3 The basic system of selecting and appointing cadres

China's cadre selection and appointment system includes three main aspects. One is the working system of cadre selection and appointment, which provides the basic methods and procedures of selecting and appointing cadres, such as *Working Regulations for Selection and Appointment of Party and Government Leading Cadres*, the selection approach to civil servants, and the relevant provisions of civil servant selection and appointment in *Civil Servant Law*. The second aspect is the assessment and evaluation system, which regulates the assessment methods and procedures of cadre performance, providing an objective basis for the selection and appointment of cadres, such as the assessment methods of the morality of cadres, the assessment methods of civil servants and the comprehensive evaluation methods of leading cadres. The third aspect is the discipline and supervision system, which regulates the disciplines abided by the relevant personnel (the selector and the selected) in the process of cadre selection and appointment and the effective supervision measures and procedures of cadre selection and appointment, such as 'On Strengthening the Supervision of the Selection and Appointment of Cadres' and 'The Accountability Measures of the Selection and Appointment of Leading Cadres of the Party and Government'.

Column2-1 The basic functions of the Organization Department

China's selection and appointment of cadres puts great emphasis on the principle of cadres under the leadership of the CPC. Specifically, party committees at all levels and their subordinate organizations are responsible for the selection and appointment of cadres. Since China has many cadres, the orderly and effective management of this team is directly correlated with the establishment and operation of the Organization Department.

The Organization Department is the main functional department to select and appoint cadres, which implements all aspects of the process from cadre selection schemes to the inspection and appointment of cadres. In addition to selection and appointment, the Organization Department is also responsible for the education and training, supervision and management, and assessment and evaluation of cadres. The management policies of cadres are also formulated by the Organization Department.

The establishment of the Organization Department of the CPC Central Committee can be traced back to the early years of the CPC. In 1925, the fourth National Congress of the CPC passed 'Resolution on Organization Issues', stating that "the new Central Committee should pay special attention to the establishment of a strong Organization Department of the CPC Central Committee, which gives real guidance to local party organizations." This 'resolution' also requires the local executive committee to set up a corresponding Organization Department, one of the central works of which is to assign party personnel to the right position. The establishment of specialized organization departments provides a solid guarantee to the management work of cadres.

The Central Organization Department, subordinate to the Central Committee of the CPC, is an important functional organization responsible for the management of all party cadres, central of which is to make the macro policy of cadre management. In terms of selection and appointment, the Central Organization Department is responsible for the selection and appointment of cadres administrated by the Central Committee of the CPC, including provincial- and ministry-level cadres, the person in charge of colleges and universities administrated by the Central Committee of the CPC, SOEs, and professional and technical units.

In parallel with the Organization Department under the Party Committee, administrative bodies also set up their own personnel departments, which are mainly responsible for the selection and management of civil servants, professional and technical personnel and other government personnel. Personnel work is carried out under the Organization Department of the Party Committee, and the chief of the personnel department is often also the deputy chief of Organization Department.

The office building of the Organization Department of the CPC Central Committee

(1) Selection and appointment system

1 'Working Regulations for Selection and Appointment of Leading Party and Government Cadres'

Working Regulations for Selecting and Appointing Leading Party and Government Leading Cadres mainly applies to the selection of leading cadres of party committees and government offices. In 1995, the CPC Central Committee promulgated *Interim Working Regulations for Selecting and Appointing Leading Party and Government Cadres*. In July 2002, the CPC Central Committee formally promulgated the regulations, which were revised on January 14, 2014. As the CPC's basic rules covering cadre selection and appointment, the 'working regulations' construct the basic framework of cadre selection and appointment as well as the mechanism of cadre management and supervision. The 'working regulations' include specific and strict rules on the basic principles, basic program, basic methods, expansion of democracy, and strengthening of supervision in leading cadre selection and appointment. The basic spirit of the regulations is to carry out the theoretical guidance of the CPC and adhere to the principle of cadres under the leadership of the CPC to ensure the correct selection of cadres applying a scientific system, democratic methods, rigorous procedures and strict discipline, so as to equip leading party and government bodies at all levels.[1]

The 'working regulations' contain 13 chapters and 71 provisions, including the guiding philosophy and basic principles on selecting and appointing leading party and government cadres; the requirements and necessary procedures of cadre selection; the regulations on cadre job exchange and avoidance; regulations on the removal, resignation and demotion of cadres, and the discipline and supervision of cadre selection and appointment.

2 'Civil Servant Law of the PRC'

The *Civil Servant Law of the PRC* was passed at the 15th session of the standing committee of the 10th NPC and implemented in January 2006. It was a milestone event in that it was the first law of the general constitution of cadre and personnel management in China. As the basic law of civil servant management, the *Civil Servant Law* stipulates the basic principles and system of civil servant management, providing an important basis for the scientific, democratic and lawful management of civil servants. The law guarantees the

---

[1] Bureau One of Cadres of the Organization Department of the CPC Central Committee. *A Study Guidance to Working Regulations for Selection and Appointment of Party and Government Leading Cadres*. Beijing: Party Construction Reading Press, 2002, p.32

right of cadres to administer in accordance with the law, which is also a support for the establishment of a professional civil servant team.[2] In 1993, the State Council promulgated *The Provisional Regulations on State Civil Servants*.

The Civil Servant Law of the PRC contains 18 chapters and 107 provisions, including regulations on civil servant recruitment; appointment and dismissal; promotion and demotion; exchange and avoidance; resignation and dismissal; and position engagement In accordance with *The Civil Servant Law*, the recruitment of chief clerks and equivalent, non-leadership positions should adopt the policies of public examination, strict inspection, equal competition and meritocracy. The employment of civil servants of central bodies and their directly affiliated organs shall be organized by the responsible departments of the central government. The employment of local civil servants at all levels are handled by the responsible organs of provincial civil service organizations and, if necessary, the responsible organs of the provincial civil service authorities can be authorized by municipal (and their district) civil service departments. *The Civil Servant Law* also provides regulations for position engagement according to which government bodies may adopt the engagement system to the employment of highly specialized positions and auxiliary positions authorized by the responsible bodies at provincial level. The employment of civil servants can adopt the civil servant recruitment procedures of public examination; for positions with relatively few applicants, suitable known or referred candidates can also be directly employed.

3 'Measures for the Public Selection of Civil Servants (Provisional)'

Public selection of civil servants refers to the appointment of civil servants at above-municipal level (above-prefecture level) bodies from lower bodies. In January 2013, the Organization Department of the CPC Central Committee and the Ministry of Population and Social Security jointly issued *Measures for the Public Selection of Civil Servants (Provisional)*. Public selection of civil servants involves selecting staff who meet the requirements of the relevant departments from those who already obtained the qualifications of civil servants. It is an important means of government personnel selection, and also one of the ways for civil servants to exchange and transfer positions.

---

[2] Bureau One of Cadres of the Organization Department of the CPC Central Committee, Bureau of Civil Servants. *Compilation of Policies and Regulations Regarding Civil Servant Law*, Beijing: Press of Chinese Personnel and Party Construction Reading Press, 2008, p.26

Measures for the Public Selection of Civil Servants (Provisional) contains eight chapters and 36 provisions, providing the qualifications, basic procedures, selection methods, discipline and supervision for those who participate in the public selection of civil servants. It is clearly stipulated that examination is the way to select civil servants openly, and they should be carried out according to the level and category of positions. The examination consists of a written examination and interview, which are organized and implemented by the responsible departments of civil servants and the organizations launching public selection, respectively.

(2) The assessment and evaluation system

1 Assessment of the morality of cadres

For the implementation of the employment standard of 'selection according to morality and talent, with morality before talent' and the establishment of the correct orientation in selection and appointment, the Organization Department of the CPC Central Committee promulgated *Guidance on Strengthening the Moral Assessment of Cadres*, which explicitly regulates the strengthening of assessment on the political quality and moral character of leading cadres.

'Guidance' mainly provides the basic requirements of cadres, the evaluation methods of cadres, and the application of assessment results in selection, appointment, training, education, supervision, management and other aspects. The moral assessment of cadres should embody the professional characteristics of national public servants and their responsibility, which should also adhere to the requirement of political integrity, progressiveness and exemplary standards. Loyalty to the party, service to the people and self-discipline are the focus, and political quality and moral character are also emphasized. Of these, the assessment on political quality of cadres mainly focuses on political orientation, political affiliation, political attitude, political discipline, as well as the party spirit and principle of cadres, focusing on whether they have firm ideals and faith; whether they adhere to the Chinese socialist road, theory and system; whether they remain loyal to the party, the nation and the people; whether they implement 'Scientific Outlook on Development'; whether they carry out the party's guidelines and policies; whether they establish the correct outlook on the world, power and career; whether they fulfill the purpose of the party; whether they stick to exercising power for the people and maintain close ties with the masses; and whether they stand to principle and dare to preside over and implement democratic centralism. The assessment of moral character mainly addresses social morality, occupational ethics, personal morality and family virtue of cadres, focusing on whether they put the socialist core value system into practice, whether they comply with social morality and resist uncivilized behavior; whether they are dedicated to work and forge ahead; whether they remain fair and upright, honest and trustworthy, well-conducted and decent; whether they comply with the behavioral standard of clean governance of equality and unselfishness, and set strict requirements to their spouses, children and other relatives.

2 Annual assessment of cadres

The results of the annual assessment are an important basis for cadre selection and appointment. In 2009, the Organization Department of CPC Central Committee formulated *The Annual Assessment Methods of Leading Party and Government Cadres (Provisional)*, which contains 15 provisions, regulating the applicable objects, assessment contents, assessment methods, basic procedures and application of assessment results.

The main content of the annual assessment is work performance, moral performance and actual achievements. The annual assessment of the leading group of cadres is mainly to evaluate functional performance, including the actual results of ideological and political construction, level of leadership, work achievements, completion of key tasks and anti-corruption campaign. The annual individual assessment of leading party and government cadres is mainly to evaluate their annual individual performance of position duties, including their actual performance in morality, ability, effort, achievement and honesty with an annual work report and test comprising the form of assessment.

This *Methods* is mainly applicable to the annual assessment of party and government leadership and its members (the responsible cadres of local party committees or government agencies). The annual assessment of those in internal bodies of the party and government along with common civil servants is implemented in accordance with the *Civil Servant Assessment Regulations (Provisional)*.

Civil Servant Assessment Regulations (Provisional) were promulgated by the Organization Department of the CPC Central Committee and the State Ministry of Personnel in 2007. They comprise six chapters and 31 provisions, including the assessment content and standard, assessment procedures, the application of the assessment results and assessment management. The principles of civil servant assessment are objectivity, fairness and a focus on actual achievements. Proceeding in accordance with the prescribed authority, requirements, standards and procedures, a combination of the leadership and the masses, a combination of regular assessment and periodic assessment, and a combination of qualitative methods and quantitative methods are stressed and carried out in the civil servant assessment.

3 Comprehensive assessment of cadres

Comprehensive assessment involves a comprehensive evaluation of a cadre's tenure performance, which therefore also makes it an important basis for the selection and appointment of new cadres. The results of comprehensive assessment often determine whether a cadre can keep his position or be promoted.

In 2009, the Organization Department of the CPC Central Committee promulgated *Measures for the Comprehensive Assessment of Local Party and Government Leadership and Leading Cadres (Provisional)* and *Measures for the Comprehensive Assessment of Party and Government Leadership and Leading Cadres (Provisional)*. These two comprehensive methods of assessment management are adopted in the tenure assessment of the party and government cadres in China.

The applicable objects of *Measures for the Comprehensive Assessment of Local Party and Government Leadership and Leading Cadres (Provisional)* are leading members of above-country level (above-department level) local party committees and governments. These measures consist of 10 chapters and 46 provisions, regulating the main contents and methods, the application of assessment results, and the implementation of the assessment organization of the comprehensive assessment of the local party and government leadership and leading cadres. This regulation emphasizes the comprehensive application of assessment methods of democratic recommendation, democratic evaluation, public opinion surveys, individual interviews, performance analysis and comprehensive evaluation in order to ensure a comprehensive, objective and accurate assessment of local party and government leadership and leading cadres. This regulation also stresses that it is based on the objective evaluation of leading cadres' political integrity, ability and the performance of their duties. According to the comprehensive evaluation result, the party organization proposes opinions and suggestions concerning selection and appointment, training and education, management and supervision, and inspiration and restraint of cadres.

Measures for the Comprehensive Assessment of Party and Government Leadership and Leading Cadres (Provisional) applies to the tenure assessment of the leadership in above-country level (department level) internal bodies of party and government (such as departments, offices, agencies and other directly subordinate institutions), and the individual inspection of the promotion and appointment of leading cadres. They comprise 10 chapters and 46 provisions. Being similar to the comprehensive assessment and evaluation methods of the local party and government leadership and leading cadres, these *Measures* contain the main contents and methods of comprehensive assessment, the application of assessment results and the implementation of the organization of the assessment. Also adopting democratic recommendation, democratic evaluation, public opinion surveys, individual interviews, performance analysis and comprehensive evaluation methods, these *Measures* aim to ensure a comprehensive, objective and accurate assessment of the internal organization of the party and government's morality, ability and performance of duties.

(3) Supervision, discipline and accountability system

In the institutional framework of cadre selection and appointment in China, discipline and accountability are also very important in the supervision and management of selecting and appointing cadres. In addition to the provisions in *Working Regulations for the Selection and Appointment of Leading Party and Government Cadres*, a system for the supervision and management of selecting and appointing cadres, discipline and accountability has been specially formulated. For example, strict restrictions are set for the personal matters of leading cadres, their participation in social groups, part-time jobs in enterprises, participation in expensive training, the involvement of their spouses and relatives in business, and travel abroad for private purposes. All the above behavior is under strict supervision. In addition, a system of party regulations and provisions have been formulated, including *The Accountability Measures of the Selection and Appointment of Leading Party and Government Cadres* (2010), *Self-reflections on Work Performance before the Resignation of City and County Party Secretaries in Cadre Selection and Appointment (Provisional)* (2010), *On Strengthening the Supervision of Cadre Selection and Appointment* (2014), *Certain Provisions on Promoting the Mobility of Leadership (Provisional)* (2014), and *Regulations on Disciplinary Punishment of Chinese Communist Party* (2015), all of which comprise a set of relatively comprehensive system of supervision, management and discipline.

4 Major ways of selecting and appointing cadres

Since China has a relatively large team of cadres, what are the ways of selecting cadres of various types and at all levels? There are four ways of cadre selection and appointment: election, commission, examination and engagement.

(1) Election system

Election is a way of selecting leading personnel by means of democratic elections in accordance with the relevant laws and regulations. Currently, all levels of party committee, the Standing Committee of the NPC, government bodies, the CPPCC, along with people's organizations and mass organizations are selected through democratic election by their respective congresses or member meetings in accordance with the provisions of the relevant laws and regulations. It is party members' exercise of their democratic rights and the people's exercise of their power to elect leaders of party committees and government organs at all levels of the Party Congress and People's Congress. Carried out regularly, the election system also has a clear regulation on the tenure of leadership, five years being one tenure.

(2) Commission system

The commission system refers to a way of directly appointing leading cadres by the appointment and dismissal bodies within administrative limit. Commission is an important form for appointing leading cadres of party committees and governments in China. It generally applies to the appointment of all responsible leaders of central state administrative bodies and local administrative bodies by the bodies of state power at all levels, and staff appointments by government departments. The party's organization and personnel department is responsible for the commission of leading cadres, democratic recommendation, investigation, discussion and appointment. The appointment of a cadre needs to be carried out according to strictly prescribed procedures by collective discussion.

(3) Examination system

The examination system is used to recruit cadres of party committees and government bodies, first by a statutory unified examination and then by competitive selection of those who have passed. The examination system has now been extended to public selection, competition for posts and a variety of other forms. This is a way of open enrollment – in accordance with the prescribed procedures – involving a combining of examination and inspection that is geared to society and to the internal organs of the party and government. As a competitive method, the examination system introduces a mechanism of competition in the process of selecting leading personnel, bringing competition into full play. The examination system generally consists of the following stages: recommended registration, qualification inspection, written examination, democratic evaluation, organizational investigation, discussion and public notice of appointment.

(4) Engagement system

The engagement system, a way of selecting and appointing leaders with a contract, is adopted by party committees and government agencies to appoint cadres who have a strong professional knowledge and high technical level. *Regulations on the Appointment of Cadres* stipulates that the engagement system is adopted in the appointment of leader positions of party committees and government institutions with high professional requirements, and the appointment period of which is not more than five years and where employee contracts can be renewed. The implementation of the engagement system is useful to the rational flow of leadership, helping to break through the restriction of unit, department and region.

The commission system highlights the relationship between the appointment authority and the person being appointed, the choice of which is directed by the upper to the lower, and the main social value orientation is efficiency. The election system highlights the legal relationship between the appointment authority and the person being appointed, the choice of which is directed from the lower to the upper, and the main value orientation is democracy. The examination system is a two-way choice, which is also directed by the upper to the lower, and the main social value orientation is fairness. At present, the election and commission systems are the main means of cadre selection and appointment in China, while the examination and engagement systems are important supplements. By taking a variety of means of selection and appointment applicable to different circumstances, all the above systems strive to attract outstanding potential leaders to the cause of the party and the state.

Chapter 3

The Working Principle of the Selection and Appointment of Cadres

The working principle is the guiding thought that should apply at work, which is also a macro control of specific work. The working principle of the selection and appointment of cadres is also the embodiment of the CPC's cadre line and policy, as well as the fundamental norm and basis of every aspect and the whole process of the selection and appointment of cadres, reflecting its social value orientation.

According to the historical experience of the work of cadre selection and appointment, *Regulations on the Selection and Appointment of Leading Cadres of the Party and Government* (2004) summed up seven working principles, which are a valuable experience that the CPC has accumulated during the long period of revolution and construction, exerting important guiding significance for the construction of ruling party cadres. At the same time, these seven principles are an organic whole whose basic spirit and requirements are reflected in all aspects of the selection and appointment of cadres.

1. Cadres under the leadership of the CPC

Cadres under the leadership of the CPC, which means that the Central Committee of the CPC and party organizations at all levels are responsible for the selection, appointment and comprehensive management of party cadres, is the main characteristic and the fundamental principle of the selection and appointment of cadres in China.

For a ruling party, the power to promote and demote staff is the most important power. Both western political parties and the ruling party of socialist countries attach great importance to the selection and use of cadres, and they all firmly hold this power in their hands. In China, the CPC is the ruling party, which in addition to its organizations at all levels should always grasp the power to select and appoint cadres, managing and supervising cadres effectively.

Cadres under the CPC's leadership is one of the most basic and important management experiences for cadre managers, which are reflected in the following two aspects:

- The CPC Central Committee is responsible for the formulation of the fundamental and specific policies of cadre management. The guidelines, principles and policies of national cadre and personnel work must be formulated by the CPC Central Committee, and the major reform measures for the selection and appointment of cadres and its comprehensive management must also be decided and approved by the CPC Central Committee.

  On carrying out the cadre management policies of the CPC Central Committee, the local or departmental party committee is allowed to formulate specific implementation measures in accordance with their actual situation. Consistency with the guidelines and policies of the CPC Central Committee is indispensable.

- As the main authority and executive body of the selection and appointment of cadres, party committees at all levels decide on leading cadre selection and appointment at the correspondent level with organization departments playing the role of functional departments, which undertake specific tasks. However, party committees at all levels must exercise the authority of selecting and appointing cadres within the prescribed limits of cadre management, and at the same time preside over its supervision and administration.

  With regard to cadre selection and appointment, 'cadres under the leadership of the CPC' are to effectively exert the leadership of party organizations in the process of motion, democratic recommendation, investigation, discussion and appointment as well as in tasks involving lawful recommendation, nomination, democratic consultation, supervision and inspection to ensure that the leadership at all levels is in the hands of those who are loyal to the party, the people and Marxism.

In China, an embodiment of 'cadres under the leadership of the CPC' is the combination of cadre recommendation by party committee and the lawful election, appointment and dismissal by organs of state authority. The recommendation of the central and local committee is an important guarantee for realizing the leadership of the CPC towards state affairs, manifesting the status of the ruling party in national political life. It is also an important duty of party committees. In fact, it is a significant authority given by the constitution for state power bodies to elect and decide the appointment and dismissal of leading cadres of state bodies.

In strengthening the responsibilities of CPC organizations in cadre selection and appointment, the CPC Central Committee has also developed a variety of systems and regulations on inner party democratic decision-making, supervision and management, responsibility and investigation, preventing deviations and violations of party organizations in the process of cadre selection and appointment.

For example, a necessary procedure in this process is democratic recommendation, which indicates that each ordinary party member has the right to recommend cadres for party organizations. In other words, the selection and appointment of cadres is completely based on democratic procedures. Taking another example, the selection and appointment of cadres should go through the collective discussion of party committees, giving full play to democracy within the party so as to avoid power abuse by an individual or a minority. In addition, the selection of cadres should be announced to the whole of society before the final appointment to ensure that every ordinary party member and citizen has the right to know, participate in, choose and supervise the selection and appointment of cadres. Moreover, party committees should deliver annual work reports on cadre selection and appointment to all party members, receiving evaluation and supervision from them. Finally, a series of relevant provisions on responsibility and punishment have been implemented (in 2016, the CPC Central Committee promulgated and implemented *The Accountability Regulations of the CPC*), to strengthen the responsibility of party organizations regarding cadre selection and appointment. Once wrongly appointed, the relevant party committee and Organization Department should shoulder the political responsibility.

2 Selection according to merit from all corners of the country

'Selection according to merit from all corners of the country' is an excellent tradition of the CPC's cadre selection and appointment and an inevitable requirement of the CPC's nature and tenet. The CPC is a political party representing the most extensive interests of the Chinese people with serving the people as its tenet. In this sense, 'selection according to merit from all corners of the country' answers the questions of 'where to select' and 'how to select' in cadre selection and appointment.

Comrade Mao Zedong once said: "Throughout our national history there have been two sharply contrasting lines on the subject of the use of cadres, one being 'appointment on merit' and the other 'appointment by favoritism'. The former is the honest and the latter the dishonest way" (from *The Role of the CPC in National War*, October 14, 1938, in volume two of *Selected Works of Mao Zedong*). It is an important problem concerning party guidelines, concepts and methods whether to appoint cadres on merit or by favoritism. Unquestionably, 'selection according to merit from all corners of the country' is the line that our party should adhere to, and it is clearly stated in *Regulations on Party and Government Cadre Selection and Appointment*. The 10th regulation proposes that the vision and channel of cadre selection should be broadened so that leading cadres can be selected from both inside and outside party organs. Attention should be paid to the selection of leading personnel from those who have served in county organs or SOEs to promote cadre exchange.

Adhering to 'selection according to merit from all corners of the country' in practice is to value the cause of our party and the merit of cadres, breaking the restrictions of personal emotion, geographical division and differences in work background, so that various talents can be found and deployed effectively.

The CPC Central Committee has gained considerable experience in the coverage and representativeness of cadre selection. For example, members of the same collective leadership and leading cadres in key positions should be more balanced in terms of work experience, age and background. Efforts should be made to achieve complementary advantages rather than having 'uniform' background or qualifications. In terms of the exchange of cadres, special attention should be paid to the overall planning, looking at every front and every region, especially cadres from difficult and complex areas. Therefore, the Central Organization department has specifically developed the system of public selection of civil servants, enriching central and local party organizations as well as government agencies with outstanding young civil servants from grassroots units.

The CPC Central Committee has also actively introduced the competition mechanism into cadre selection work, implementing, to a certain extent, public selection and appointment and competition in order to increase competitive selection and ensure a smooth channel for outstanding cadres. *Regulations on Party and Government Cadre Selection and Appointment* has made very specific provisions on the ways of handling the competition system and public selection. In addition, the selection of cadres in government agencies and departments is not limited to CPC members; in fact, a considerable proportion of officials are not CPC party members but instead are members of other parties or have no party affiliation. Moreover, the proportion of female cadres in central and local party and government organizations is gradually increasing.

Column3-1 The system of public selection of civil servants in China

The public selection of civil servants is the mechanism of training and selection specifically established to optimize the structure of leading cadres, which is a concrete manifestation of the principle of 'selection according to merit from all corners of the country'. From 2013, the public selection of civil servants has been organized by the Organization Department of the CPC Central Committee and the Ministry of Human Resources and Social Security.

The public selection of civil servants means that cadres can be selected from lower organs to higher municipal (prefecture) level organs. This is not only an important way to improve the quality of cadres and to enrich the experience of primary staff, but also provides a significant channel for primary civil servants to be promoted to higher authorities. There are two types of public selection: parallel transfer and promotion. The former refers to a transfer to higher authorities by selection, but with the rank and position unchanged. The latter refers to a transfer to higher authorities by selection with position or rank promoted. Those who participate in public selection of civil servants should have more than two years' work experience at grassroots party organizations.

Each year the CPC Central Committee, state organs and ministries, and municipal party committees and government agencies, regularly carry out public selection of civil servants. The procedures of public selection are as follows: (1) announcement, (2) registration and qualification examination, (3) examination, (4) organizational inspection, and (5) decision and appointment.

Examination has replaced the conventional way of recommendation in public cadre selection and appointment. In accordance with the regulations, public selection is used when no candidate is qualified for a particular position in higher-ranking organs, and when there is a need for people with grassroots experience. Also, due to fact that many people take part in public selection, recommendation as a way of selection is unmanageable, which makes examination possible and, indeed, inevitable. However, examination results are not the only factor in determining the selection of personnel; other factors such as political quality, professional morality, work ability and work experience are indispensable.

In 2016, 61 institutions of the party's central organs and state government departments provided positions including director, deputy director, researcher, deputy researcher, principal staff member, senior staff member and clerk for public selection, and 521 civil servants were selected. Compared with the previous year when 54 agencies publicly selected 400 civil servants, the size of 2016 selection increased unprecedentedly. Besides, party organizations and government departments at or above the municipal level have greatly enlarged the scale of public selection, which provides more opportunities for grassroots talent to work in central organs and facilitate their promotion.

3. Selection according to morality and talent with morality before talent

This principle answers the question of 'who to select', which is the basic standard of cadre selection and appointment in China, as well as the concentrated expression and core content of the CPC's cadre management.

Morality refers to the political quality and moral character of cadres, including theoretical ability of politics, basic thoughts, ideals and beliefs, political stance and orientation, political discipline, social morality, professional morality, personal morality, family virtue, as well as judicial administration and clean governance. Talent refers to the professional and leadership ability of cadres, including ability of knowledge, profession, organization and coordination, decision-making and the ability to solve practical problems. As for the relationship between morality and talent, the CPC always adheres to the unification of the doctrine that everything has two aspects and that everything has its key points. In this sense, both morality and talent are indispensable, but morality is the priority. On the one hand, morality is like the commander of talent, determining the role and direction of talent. On the other hand, talent supports morality, affecting the scope of morality. It is difficult for cadres who are virtuous but not competent to bear responsibility. Conversely, a talent without morality will eventually destroy the party's ability to govern. Therefore, CPC selection and appointment always values the talent of cadres, but at the same time attention is also paid to the morality of cadres, with the latter preceding the former.

In 2013, at the National Organization meeting, the General Secretary of the CPC Central Committee, Xi Jinping, proposed that cadres should be "strong in belief, caring for the people, diligent and pragmatic, responsible and accountable, and honest and upright", which enriches and develops the present connotation of the standard as 'selection according to morality and talent with morality before talent'. Among these attributes, a firm political belief is the most important standard of cadre selection, and it comprises the core of the 'morality' of cadres. In today's China when reform and opening up is going through difficult times, it is of primary importance to select outstanding cadres who are politically reliable and competent.

- Cadres should be politically reliable, meaning they should adhere to the correct political direction; firmly take the socialist road with Chinese characteristics; resolutely implement the basic theory, basic line, basic program, basic experience as well as policies; be consciously and highly consistent with the CPC Central Committee; distinguish right from wrong on major issues of principle; pass crucial tests and overcome various difficulties; maintain absolute loyalty to the party; and strive to serve the people wholeheartedly.

- Cadres should be competent, meaning they should be diligent and hardworking, possessing knowledge and ability in their own work. They should also have a dialectical and material way of thinking and working, insisting on emancipating the mind, seeking truth from facts and keeping pace with the times, combining the party's lines, principles, and policies with local conditions. They are also required to work in accordance with a scientific outlook on development and establish a correct view of achievements in order to lead and create outstanding achievements in innovation practice of reform and opening up.

The morality and talent of cadres should be grasped in the inspection of their actual performance in daily work, study and life, as well as their performance at crucial moments and key events, seeing whether they are firm in political stance, decent in morality, and competent in work and leadership.

4. Selection according to achievements and public recognition

This principle is mainly to answer the question of 'what are the criteria of cadre selection'. In other words, it is the basic method of selecting and appointing cadres in China, and is embodied in its whole process.

Morality and talent are subjective, while achievements are objective. Achievements are the actual effectiveness of cadres in fulfilling their duties, which are an objective reflection of cadres' quality of morality and talent in practice. Adhering to the principle of achievements is to set achievements in an important position in the process of cadre selection and appointment, so that the performance of cadres' duty and the effectiveness of their service can be analyzed and evaluated comprehensively, historically and dialectically. Adherence to the principle of public view is to follow the mass line, promote democracy and fully believe and rely on the masses in the task of cadre selection, so that cadres who get most support are selected.

To carry out this principle, we should, first of all, view the actual achievements of cadres as the important basis and recognize it as the guiding role in the process of cadre selection and appointment. To some extent, the rapid development of China's economic construction as well as reform and opening up have been driven by the implementation of this principle. The growth and progress of cadres in politics and actual work are shown in the outstanding achievements they have made. By focusing on this principle, those who have made outstanding achievements and have gained innovative experience during reform and opening up will have a greater chance of promotion, thus creating a benign performance-orientation environment. Central and local party organizations should pay special attention to a comprehensive, historical and general grasp of the achievements of cadres, while never ignoring the external environment; therefore, cadres' achievements must be judged, analyzed and evaluated scientifically. In practical work, China also absorbs and draws lessons from the method of performance evaluation in the management of human resources and strives to evaluate cadres' performance objectively and scientifically.

In the practice of cadre selection and appointment, emphasis is put on the dialectical unity between morality and performance. The morality and talent of cadres are the premise of their performance, which determines whether they can attain significant achievements, while achievements are the result of an interaction between morality, talent and the environment. In other words, achievement is the physical form of morality and talent as well as their reflection under certain conditions. There is an inevitable connection between morality, talent and political achievement, which should never be separated. The Central Organization Department specially formulated *Proposed Regulations Reflecting the Requirements of the Scientific Outlook on Development about the Comprehensive Evaluation of Leading Local Party and Government Cadres*, which demands a full understanding of the local economic and social development, the evaluation and opinion of the masses, and a full understanding of the local development in a particular period of time, so that focus could be put on the analysis of the ideas, involvement and performance of leading local government bodies and leading cadres, completely reflecting the selection of cadres based on morality and talent.

Adhering to the principle of public recognition means that selection work should fully trust and rely on the masses and that democracy in work should be expanded, which encourages the masses to be more involved in the recommendation, investigation and other relevant work in order to select and appoint cadres who have won the endorsement and support of the majority. To further expand democracy in the work of cadres, the right to know, participate in, choose and supervise the selection and appointment of cadres among party members and the masses is implemented, so that the mass line is maintained and decisions made only by a minority of people are avoided. Regardless of the ways of appointment, China's organization and personnel departments at all levels adhere to the mass line and give full play to democracy, implementing democratic recommendation, opinion polls or democratic appraisal to ensure the selection of cadres who are recognized by the people as adhering to the line of reform and opening up and making significant achievements. It is necessary to point out that, in China, 'recognition of the masses' is an organizational behavior, which is realized through the party's cadre selection work (such as democratic recommendation), rather than through spontaneous public behavior or a 'referendum'.

5. Democratic, open, competitive and preferential selection

This principle answers the question of 'how to select', which is a concrete implementation of the previous focus on achievements and public recognition, and also a valuable experience in deepening the reform of the personnel system. Put simply, the major working procedures of cadre selection and appointment are all reflected in the democratic, open, competitive and preferential principle.

The democratic principle is to insist on the implementation of the right to know of party members as well as the masses, participate in, select and supervise the process of cadre selection and appointment, which could further smooth channels of public expression, normalize its procedure in order to strengthen the scientific and authentic means of public expression, and improve the quality of democracy in cadre selection. The open principle is to make the scope, positions, conditions, procedures, rules and results of cadre selection known to the public, so that the authority to select cadres is exercised transparently. The principle of competition is to let participants fully display their talents and advantages in a competition of morality, talent and achievements with normative form and unified rules and standards, so that cadres can be easily distinguished. The preferential principle is to achieve the goal of selecting the best and the strongest by comprehensive comparison and weighing.

It is out of a desire to expand the vision, broaden the channel and create a good working condition and social environment that we adopt the democratic and open principle in the selection and appointment of cadres. One important sign showing that we are carrying forward the democratic principle is to abide by the principle of democratic recommendation. Every ordinary party member along with the masses have the right to recommend cadres to the party organization. Besides conference voting and personal recommendation, there are also individual conversations, field surveys, opinion collections, etc. Democratic principle and the open principle are also reflected in the whole process of the motion, the inspection notice, communication and consultation, discussion and decision, publicity before appointment. In the work of cadre selection and cadre deployment, democracy is the means but not the ends, and it is only one of the ways to select and make full use of cadres.

The implementation of the competitive principle and preferential principle is to select the best talent, solving the problem of 'only promotion but no demotion' so that the normal metabolic system of the cadre team can be established. But what needs to be pointed out is that competition is not the same as election, in the sense that competition is to create a strong prerequisite for selecting the best. That is why we need to standardize and perfect the selection methods, improving the scientific level of selection. One of the most important experiences is that we should not simply let vote or exam decide cadre selection as has been recorded in the revised *Regulations on Party and Government Cadre Selection and Appointment* by the CPC Central Committee in 2015. In fact, the western experience of electing leaders has fully demonstrated that vote is not necessarily equivalent to competence. For most posts selected by the system of appointment, the principle of democracy, openness, competition and preference must be implemented in order to avoid the selection of cadres being concentrated in the hands of just a few people. But democracy and competition are diverse and can be realized in many ways. In China, one of the most important experiences is to combine the party's leadership and democracy and let party organizations play the leading role and supervise cadre selection and management.

6 Democratic centralism

The principle of democratic centralism is the basic organization and leadership system of the CPC, which is the guarantee for correctly implementing the party's cadre policies and making cadre work scientific, democratic and institutionalized.

Generally speaking, democracy is a legitimate expression of the wishes and opinions of party organizations, cadres and the masses regarding cadre appointment, while concentration is the final expression of the will of cadres and the masses. Democracy is the premise and foundation of concentration, while concentration is the inevitable requirement and result of democracy. The experience of the selection and management of Chinese cadres is that we must correctly grasp and deal with the dialectical relationship between democracy and centralism, and adhere to the combination of centralism based on democracy and democracy under centralized guidance.

While adhering to democratic centralism in the work of cadre selection and appointment, we should firstly emphasize full democracy, improving democratic quality and continuously exploring effective forms of democracy. The democracy of cadre selection and appointment is mainly reflected in the whole process of proposal, democratic recommendation, investigation, discussion and decision, appointment, nomination by law and democratic consultation. Moreover, we should also adhere to the collective leadership system. Concentration is not the realization or imposition of personal will. The final decision of the selection and appointment of cadres at all levels is given to the collective leadership of party organizations; party organizations at all levels (mainly party committees) decide the appointment and dismissal of cadres by discussion.

In practice, following the requirement of 'collective leadership, democratic centralism, individual consultation and conference decision', party committees at all levels should carefully weigh up an appointment before final announcement, and seek the views of different parties in order to ensure that the cadres selected are well known. At the same time, party committees should focus on improving and perfecting the rules of discussion and decision-making procedures in deciding the appointment and dismissal of cadres, so that the leading role and supervision function of party committees (party organization) are fully displayed. No one is allowed to act above the party organization. During the selection process, stresses are put on the decision-making role of the Party Congress and the committee. Specifically, the candidates for the party's chief leadership at municipal and county rank should be nominated by a higher ranked party committee, discussed by all committee members of the corresponding municipal and county rank, and finally decided by secret ballot.

7 Principle of acting by law

This principle is to answer the question of 'how to combine the principle of cadres under the leadership of the CPC in compliance with laws and regulations'. Adhering to the principle of acting by law is the embodiment of the CPC Central Committee's strategy of governing the country by law and the general goal of the construction of a socialist country under the rule of law in the work of cadre management, which requires not only an institutionalized and standardized cadre management but also a connection with national laws and regulations and other regulations within the party. In other words, the work of cadre management should be acted within the refinements of the law.

Generally speaking, acting by law in cadre selection and appointment requires party committees at all levels and organization and personnel departments at all levels to act both in accordance with the principles, standards, procedures and discipline formulated in *Regulations on Party and Government Cadre Selection and Appointment* and the provisions of state laws and regulations. Specifically, for the management of selected cadres, the principle of cadres under the leadership of the CPC and the principle of acting by law should be combined.

Column3-2 The selection system in cadre selection and appointment

The selection system is a system of determining leadership by voting in accordance with the provisions of relevant laws and regulations, which currently is one of the major forms of the appointment of cadres. All levels of party committee, the Standing Committee of the NPC and people's congresses at all levels, government organs, the CPPCC, and people's organizations and mass organizations are all selected through election by their respective congresses or member meetings in accordance with the provisions of the relevant laws and regulations.

Positions belonging to the selection system include:

- *Positions selected in accordance with The Constitution of the CPC: members, secretary and deputy secretary of the standing committee of local committees at all levels; members of the standing committee, secretary and deputy secretary of the Discipline Inspection Commission at all levels.*

- *Positions selected and appointed according to state laws: director, deputy-director, secretary and committee member of the standing committee of people's congresses above county level, as well as the director member, deputy-director member and member of the specific committee.*

- *The staff of government agencies at all levels selected and appointed according to the legal provisions of the state, including ministers of the State Council, directors of general committees, the president of the People's Bank of China, the auditor general and chief secretary; as well as staff in local government agencies at all levels, such as the governors and deputy governors, chairman and vice chairmen of autonomous regions, the mayor and deputy mayor, governors of autonomous prefectures, vice governors of autonomous states, governor and deputy governors of the county, district chief and vice district chief, chief secretary, directors of the general departments, bureau director, committee director, chief and section chief.*

- *Staff in judicial and procuratorial organs selected and appointed in accordance with the legal provisions of the state, including president and vice president of the local people's court, the judge, vice judge, members of the judicial committee, judicial officer and chief procurator of the local people's procuratorate, deputy chief procurator, members of the Procuratorial Committee and the procurator.*

- *Posts selected in accordance with the* Regulations on the People's Political Consultative Conference, *including the chairman, vice chairman and chief secretary general of CPPCC local committees at all levels.*

Elections are usually carried out regularly, and there is always a clear regulation regarding the term of office of the leaders, each term being five years, and the longest term of office in the same position should be no more than 10 years.

The fifth provision of *Regulations on Party and Government Cadre Selection and Appointment* requires that recommended and nominated candidates should follow its principles, standards and procedures, but the selection, appointment and demotion of those posts should follow state laws and regulations, which, in this sense fully embodies the organic combination of the principle of cadres under the leadership of the CPC and the principle of acting by law.

Besides the seven basic principles mentioned above, China's selection and appointment of cadres also attaches great importance to the training and selection of young cadres, emphasizing a grassroots orientation.

Regulations on Party and Government Cadre Selection and Appointment emphasizes the training and selection of outstanding young cadres, the use of reserve cadres (see below) and the use of cadres of all ages. The training and selection of outstanding young cadres is associated with the constant development of the party's cause and the nation's long-term peace and stability. That is why party organizations at all levels have always attached great importance to this principle. Therefore, with training as the basis, wise choice and appropriate appointment as the foundation, and strict management as the guarantee, we should constantly improve the selection mechanism of the training of young cadres and strive to achieve normalized training, reasonable equipment and institutionalized operation, so that a sufficient number of young cadres that come from various sources and have reasonable structure and excellent quality can be built. What needs to be stressed is that the attention we have attached to the selection of young cadres does not mean that every cadre promoted or appointed should be young or every team should be equipped with young cadres, or an even that age descends from high to low positions. In specific work, we emphasize an upholding of the fine tradition of combining old leadership with the middle-aged and young, so that a reasonable echelon structure of leaders can be constructed.

China's cadre selection and appointment system also implements a system of reserve cadres. Reserve cadres are those outstanding cadres with morality, talent and potential that are selected as candidates prepared for future leadership within the cadre management authority and in accordance with the relevant standards and processes of selection. The basic principle of selecting and training cadres is to control the scale, optimize the structure and simplify the procedures so as to select those outstanding cadres who are moral, talented, highly performing, widely recognized and with great potential into our team of cadre reserves. Reserve cadres are usually under the rule of party organizations and where a mechanism of dynamic management, talent survival, training, timely use, regular adjustment, free promotion and demotion is adopted.

Cadre selection and appointment in China focuses on grassroots orientation, which is dedicated to continuously improving the structure of the sources of cadre experience, enabling cadres to understand the local and state situation, cultivate emotion towards the masses, establish the view of the masses, and strengthen the ability to handle complex problems.

In specific work, the grassroots unit is regarded as the main field to train and educate cadres, in which cadres can accumulate experience, improve their ability and mature. At the same time, more attention is attached to grassroots experience in cadre selection and cadre use, so that a large number of outstanding cadres with grassroots experience are selected and appointed to the leadership of the party and government organs at all levels. In other words, cadres as a whole know about the reform practice of the grassroots, which provides a guarantee of talent for the development and progress of China's reform and opening up.

Chapter 4

Compulsory Procedures of the Selection and Appointment of Cadres

The selection and appointment of cadres should follow specific working procedures. During the long revolutionary struggle and construction, the CPC established a set of effective procedures for the selection and appointment of cadres, which not only adheres to the basic principles of cadres under the leadership of the CPC, but also reflects the concept of cadre selection and appointment that is objective and fair, focuses on achievements and values recognition from the masses, and therefore should be strictly followed. In general, the promotion and appointment of cadres should follow the five processes of motion, democratic recommendation, investigation, decision through discussion and appointment.

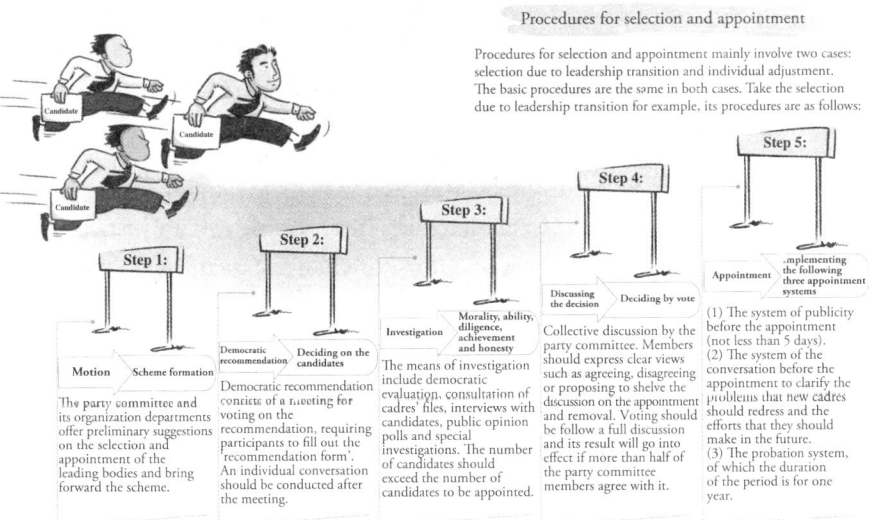

Graphic 4-1: Basic procedures of cadre selection and appointment in China
(Source: Website of the Department of Outreach of the CPC Central Committee www.idcpc.org.cn)

1 Motion

Motion refers to the process of starting the work of cadre selection and appointment as well as forming the working program by the party committee or its subordinate organizations and personnel department within the authority of the management of cadres. It is the initial stage of cadre selection, and to a large extent it determines the direction and result of selection and appointment work. Motion should be set at an initial position in order to implement the basic principles of cadres under the leadership of the CPC, and highlight the leading and supervising function of party organizations, so that the four processes followed could be connected, making the whole process complete and standardized, and providing the basis for supervision and inspection.

(1) The subject and timing of the motion process

The newest revised version of *Regulations on the Selection and Appointment of Leading Cadres of the Party and Government* in 2015 puts forward that the main body to start cadre selection and appointment is the general party committee or its subordinate organization and personnel departments (the party organ in charge is the Organization Department; the government agency in charge is the Personnel Department). Motion opinions may take oral or written forms and should be based on the needs of the work and the construction of the leadership team. Generally speaking, the motion starts when the term of leadership or institution changes, or when there is leadership vacancy, a need to optimize leadership structure, or a need for post rotation and the avoidance of closely related people from working in the same department.

The motion process cannot be initiated when: the main leadership of an organization has made it clear that they intend to leave; an institution is under reform; the administrative relationship changes; or the agency's cadres have fulfilled the position quota.

The term 'position quota' refers to the number of cadre posts determined by the central or local organization and institution management departments for all party and government agencies, which is commonly known as the 'three regulation programs': the regulation of department responsibilities, the regulation of internal organs and the regulation of staffing, of which the last two regulations include the number of cadre posts needed. In China, the number of cadres at all levels of party and government are set and cannot be broken in the selection and appointment of cadres.

(2) The ways and results of the motion process

When it is time for cadre selection and appointment, party committees or organization and personnel departments will put forward opinions on initiating cadre selection and appointment in accordance with their power and the needs of the post. Based on relevant suggestions and situations grasped during normal times, the organization and personnel departments propose a preliminary suggestion on position, condition, scope, methods and procedures of cadre selection and appointment, which will finally develop into a work plan after reporting to the chief leadership of the party committees (Leading Party Group) and careful 'brewing'.

In China's cadre selection and appointment, 'brewing' is an important approach in adhering to democratic centralism, giving full play to democracy. 'Brewing' refers to the process in which responsible leaders of party committees or organization and personnel departments start a preliminary proposal on the work plan about cadre selection and appointment, which is then followed by communication, consultation and advice to a limited extent. In so doing, we can ensure the authority of the party committees, and prevent a possible misuse of power by an individual or minority. 'Brewing' usually takes the form of meetings or individual discussions. The participants are usually the relevant superior leadership or leadership team members.

The final result of the motion is the formation of the work plan on cadre selection and appointment, including the position, conditions, scope, methods and procedures involved.

Column 4-1: The authority limit of cadre management

The authority limit of cadre management refers to the scope of authority and responsibility of the CPC Central Committee and local party committees at all levels, which has had different provisions in different historical periods since the founding of the New China. Before 1983, the CPC Central Committee and local party committees at all levels were in charge of leading cadres of two-rank lower institutions. From 1984, in order to adapt to the reform of the economic system and promote the development of cadre teams, the Central Organization Department, with the principle of 'less control, flexible management and better administration', delegated cadre management authority from the two-ranking management to the one-ranking management that is still used today. 'One-ranking management' means that the CPC Central Committee is responsible for the management of central and state organs (including the chief leadership of the People's Court, the People's Procuratorate and the Disciplinary Committee of the party), as well as leading cadres at ministries and provincial autonomous regions and municipalities directly under the central government. Moreover, the provincial party committees, in principle, are responsible for leading cadres at prefecture (department) level, but some chief leaders of the party and government organs at county level (municipal) are also in the charge of the provincial party committee.

With the basic principles determined by the CPC Central Committee, party committees develop their own list of official positions under their management and determine the specific scope of management authority, within which cadre appointment and dismissal are decided, nominated or recommended. Those cadres who should be selected and appointed in accordance with the selection system or whose appointment needs to fulfill corresponding legal regulations or procedures, should be elected by law.

Some institutions are subject to dual management by the relevant departments of the central and local party organizations. The investigation, appointment or dismissal of their cadres are generally headed by the chief management organization; the co-management organization is only involved in part of the selection work.

2 Democratic recommendation

Article 14 of *Regulations on the Selection and Appointment of Leading Cadres of the Party and Government* stipulates that democratic recommendation is an indispensable process of the selection and appointment of leading party and government cadres, which best reflects the democracy of the cadre selection process.

Democratic recommendation refers to the activity of recommending leading cadres organized by party committees and their organization and personnel departments according to their needs, which should follow prescribed procedures, scope and requirements. The recommended results are an important reference for the selection and appointment of cadres, which is valid for one year.

(1) Main forms of democratic recommendation

There are two forms of democratic recommendation: meeting recommendation and individual discussion. Whether it relates to promotion after the expiration of an office term, or an individual promotion to fill a vacant position, the two forms should occur at the same time, and complement and support each other, and the results should be given comprehensive analysis before being adopted.

The meeting recommendation is a democratic recommendation meeting held by the organization and personnel departments, in which people at the meeting make recommendations according to the posts, conditions and scope stipulated by the work plan of cadre selection and appointment. Participants fill in the recommendation form from the list of qualified cadres, recommending those who could meet their expectations. Individual discussion involves the organization and personnel departments listening to the referees' opinions to a more limited extent than the meeting recommendation in order to obtain a list of recommended candidates.

In general, selection at the expiration of a leadership term first adopts the meeting recommendation and then moves on to individual discussion. As for individual promotion after the vacancy of a position, it could follow the same order of selection as above, but it may be reversed so as to ensure the quality of democratic recommendation through the organic combination of the leading role of party organizations, the basic role of public opinion and the propriety between post responsibility and the candidate's ability.

(2) Other forms of democratic recommendation

As stipulated in Articles 21 and 22 of *Regulations on the Selection and Appointment of Leading Cadres of the Party and Government*, individuals can make recommendations regarding leading cadre candidates, as can party organizations under specific circumstances.

Whether it is leading cadres, general party members, cadres or the masses, they all have the right to recommend leading cadres to party organizations. Personal recommendation must follow the conditions and qualifications of cadre selection and appointment. They should also append their signature to recommendation materials, elaborating on the morality, ability, effort, achievement and honesty of the recommended person, explaining the reasons for the recommendation, as well as their relationship with the recommended. This provision ensures the democratic rights of every ordinary CPC member or non-CPC member in the democratic recommendation of cadres.

Direct recommendation by party organizations means that, equipped with the necessary work and leadership requirements, the party committees or the organization and personnel departments directly nominate the investigated.

This is an exception of democratic recommendation and is applied only to the selection of leaders for special positions, such as national security bodies that are not suitable for democratic recommendation.

Democratic recommendation is an important procedure for the selection and appointment of cadres, since public opinion is an important factor. However, there are other ways and means to know about cadres. In practice, the result of a democratic recommendation is not regarded as the only basis to determine the degree of recognition of the masses. It should be emphasized that recommendation is not the same as election, and a recommendation vote is not equal to an electoral vote. The reason for such provisions is not only to maintain the democratic procedure of democratic recommendation, ensuring mass line as an important system in cadre selection and appointment, but also to prevent vote determination, improving the quality and authenticity of democratic recommendation, as well as solving problems such as a timidity to shoulder responsibility, or of being reticent, or even canvassing bribes to get more votes.

The result of democratic recommendation is that, based on the comprehensive analysis and assessment of recommended personnel, the organization and personnel departments propose a preliminary list of candidates for investigation in the next stage to the party committees.

3 Investigation

Investigation involves party committees and the organization and personnel departments giving comprehensive understanding and fair evaluation on the investigated within the authority limit and according to specified procedures and methods. This is not only important work to provide the basis for cadre selection and appointment, but also an indispensable procedure and key process, providing both the premise and foundation of correct selection and deployment of cadres.

(1) The determination of the investigated

After democratic recommendation, the party committees and their organization and personnel departments submit preliminary candidates to the Standing Committee. The determination of the investigated then follows, which is the key procedure of cadre selection and deployment, and also the premise of the implementation of investigation work. Based on the work needs and the morality and ability of cadres, the investigated is normally determined through comprehensive consideration and evaluation according to democratic recommendation and their regular assessment, annual assessment, consistent performance and suitability for the post.

Regulations on the Selection and Appointment of Leading Cadres of the Party and Government makes specific provisions on the ways of determining the object of investigation, which is, in general, based on the work needs and the morality and ability of cadres. It should comprehensively consider the result of democratic recommendation, the consistent performance and suitability of the cadre for the post and other factors, all of which are designed to prevent a simple association between recommendation votes and election votes. The determination of the recommended should be completely investigated, with the leading role and supervision function of the party organizations comprehensively realized.

At the end of the leadership term, the party secretary, deputy secretary and the Standing Committee in charge of organization and discipline inspection work at the same rank, with feedback from the superior party committee and organization department, will consider and evaluate the candidates and then propose a list of the investigated. After communicating with the superior party committee and organization department, the names of the investigated will be determined. As for individual promotion to fill a vacant post, the party committee will discuss and determine the investigated, whose number will usually exceed those of the cadres to be appointed.

(2) The exclusion condition of the investigated

Article 24 of *Regulations on the Selection and Appointment of Leading Cadres of the Party and Government* specifically lists those candidates who cannot be enlisted as the object of investigation, demonstrating the strict measures taken in this regard. They are as follows:

- Those whose public recognition is not high, reflected in a low vote of democratic recommendation, and poor results in the latest three years' inspection, assessment and evaluation, as well as those criticized and regarded poorly by the masses.

- Those identified as having a lower than basic level of competence in the annual assessment over the previous three years (the annual assessment usually has four competence levels: excellence, competence, basic competence and incompetence).

- Those who have been verified as striving hard for an office position in a clandestine way or canvassing votes. The former refers to those seeking a position or promotion through improper means such as using connections while the latter refers to the use of unusual means in the process of recommendation, democratic evaluation, organization investigation and election to obtain a false recommendation or recognition.

- Those whose spouses have emigrated the mainland, or, if they have no spouse, their children have emigrated. In other words, their spouse or children have obtained foreign nationality, or have received a permanent or long-term residence permit of a foreign country or territory.

- Those who are being punished by party organizations or facing disciplinary punishment by the party or government, or who have previously received any punishment or disciplinary punishment, or those who are considered unsuitable for promotion due to various reasons.

It is an important measure of the strict management of cadres to enlist exclusion provisions specifically in the system documentation of cadre selection and appointment, which is crucial to improving the quality of the object of investigation and to reinforcing the leading role of party organizations.

(3) The process and methods of investigation

The investigation of cadres is conducted by the organization or personnel department that has management authority towards the appointed positions. The investigation consists of the following seven procedures:

- To construct the investigation team and formulate investigation plans. The investigation team is formed by more than two members of the party committee or organization and personnel departments. Investigation team members need to be of high quality and have relevant qualifications, and the person in charge of the team needs to be highly qualified in politics and richly experienced in cadre selection work. The responsibility system for the investigation of cadres requires the investigation team to be fair and upright, thorough and scrupulous, truthfully reflecting the situation and opinions of the investigation, shouldering responsibility for the material on those being investigated, and fulfilling the supervision duty of cadre selection and appointment. The investigation plan includes the objectives, contents, methods, steps and disciplines of investigation work.

- To communicate with senior leaders of the party committee about the investigation plan, listen to their opinions and then adjust the content and scope of the investigation.

- To release the pre-notice of cadre investigation, including the object, time, content, contact information of the investigation, and accepting the supervision of party members and the masses.

- To conduct individual discussions, democratic evaluations, on-site visits, interviews, issue inquiry forms and access to check cadre files and work materials, and interviews in order to comprehensively understand the general condition of those being investigated. Public opinion surveys, special investigations and extended investigations are to be carried out when necessary. This process is the main stage of cadre investigation work.

- To comprehensively analyze the investigation, all the investigations should be conducted in a consistent manner, so that the evaluation is conducted thoroughly and correctly.

- To provide feedback to the chief leaders of the organization to which the investigated are recommended or the chief leaders of the organization where the investigated now work, and also exchange views with them.

- To raise an appointment proposal and report to the organization and personnel departments that sends them. After collective discussion among organization and personnel departments, the suggestion on cadre appointment should be reported to the party committee (party group).

The main methods of investigation include individual discussions, democratic evaluation, issuing inquiry forms, on-site visits, checks on cadres' files and work records, and interviews with the investigated. Individual discussions are handled in the locality or department (unit) where the investigated work or direct discussions with the investigated, the content of which is to comprehensively know the morality, ability, efforts, achievements and honesty of those being investigated. Democratic evaluation requires staff involved to complete a democratic evaluation table that is designed to provide an overall evaluation and a sub-evaluation that includes 'morality, ability, effort, achievement and honesty'. The former has four levels: excellent, competent, basically competent and incompetent. The latter also has four levels: excellent, good, fairly good and bad. The inquiry forms are issued to solicit opinions of cadres and the masses about the promotion and appointment of the investigated, which is carried out together with democratic evaluation. On-site visits are conducted to deeply understand the achievements, effects and recognition of the masses through observation, visits, inspection and the other forms of investigation. Checks on the files and work records of cadres are important basic work needed to correctly understand general information about those being investigated. After 2015, the Central Organization Department specifically stipulated new regulations (see Chapter 5) on a stricter investigation of cadres, which emphasized the serious and scrupulous checks on a cadres' working length, age, date since joining the party, education background, work experience, etc.

(4) The content of observation, on the basis of which promotion is decided

The content of the investigation answers the question of what is the basis for a cadre be promoted. In China, both selected cadres and commissioned cadres are promoted and appointed through a comprehensive evaluation based on their competence. Therefore, the investigation covers all aspects of morality, ability, effort, achievement and honesty.

The investigation of morality mainly highlights political quality and moral character. The investigation on political quality involves investigating cadre performance on political orientation, political stance, political attitude, political discipline and party spirit and principle; it focuses on determining whether cadres can hold firm ideals and faith, adhere to political discipline, uphold the principle, shoulder responsibility, carry out democratic centralism, and take criticism and self-criticism. The investigation into cadre morality evaluates social and professional morality, individual integrity and family virtue, focusing on understanding the performance of cadres in recognition of the socialist core value system, abiding by social and public morality and resisting all kinds of uncivilized behavior. Dedication, practical devotion, energetic progression, honesty, trustworthiness, uprightness and decency of taste are also included, as well as performance in compliance with clean governance, avoiding self-interest and strictly requiring their spouses, children and other relatives to comply with the above guidelines. The investigation results on cadre morality are the primary basis for the selection and appointment of cadres; the top performers will be given priority in selection.

Investigation of achievement involves assessing the actual achievements of the cadres investigated, focusing on the actual effect of fulfilling their duties, promoting and serving scientific development. For example, when investigating the leaders and chief leaders of local party and government organizations, we should thoroughly investigate the actual results of their governance, especially the impact on the construction of the economy, politics, culture, society, ecological civilization and party building, observing the achievements of their attempts to solve the contradictions and problems in development. Therefore, the quality, effectiveness and benefits of sustainable economic development, as well as the improvement of people's livelihood and social harmony and progress, cultural construction, ecological civilization construction and party building are an important content of investigation. Moreover, the employment, income, science and technological innovation, education and culture, social security, and health assessment are emphasized. Besides, the index system is strengthened, of which the index weight on the consumption of resources, environmental protection, digestion of excess capacity, production safety and debt condition are increased. The GDP and the GDP growth rate are no longer the main evaluation index for judging the performance of cadres.

The investigation of ability and effort is designed to observe and judge the competence and work style of cadres. Their ability is often reflected in their actual achievements, which should be evaluated together with the professional ability and leadership skills of cadres. In the process of competitive selection, we generally take examination and evaluation together to comprehensively grasp the competence and professional ability of cadres. The investigation of effort involves making a comprehensive evaluation of work style, to see whether leading cadres can seek truth as well as handle practical matters, whether they are keen to serve the people, and can deeply understand grassroots conditions, whether they have a strong sense of enterprise and responsibility, whether they work under their own initiative and in a diligent and enthusiastic way; and whether they keep the mass party line, and consciously oppose formalism, bureaucracy, hedonism and luxury. In actual work, cadres who could be self-disciplined, who could seek truth and remain industrious and honest will be more likely to get promoted.

The investigation of honesty is mainly to see whether leading cadres consciously abide by the provisions of clean governance, whether there has been misuse of power to seek illegitimate gain, a dishonest tendency to seek personal gain in the process of cadre selection and appointment, and whether they are strict with relatives and close staff members, and offer them no special favors.

As for those leaders in charge of honesty investigations, the effects of their education, supervision and management of the condition of clean governance to other members in the leaders' team is also investigated, which includes an investigation into whether they support the work of the discipline and inspection body.

(5) The results of the investigation

Through the comprehensive evaluation of all cadres being investigated, the investigation team will write an opinion on all of them, which will be submitted to party committees for their decision. The written comments must be realistic, comprehensive and accurate, clearly reflecting the information of the investigated, including their performance, main strengths, main shortcomings and deficiencies in morality, ability, effort and achievement, as well as a description of the democratic recommendation and assessment, including recommended ticket and comprehensive evaluation.

The investigation work should be put into a series of documents and files, which are used as a way of effective supervision in the process of cadre investigation to see whether the cadre selection and appointment work follows relevant provisions, procedures and requirements. The investigation documents and files generally include: a proposal report on investigation and investigation work plan, tables of democratic recommendation and democratic evaluation, records of important discussions, investigation report, investigation material, the application form on cadre appointment and dismissal, the important questions and results in investigation, the solicited written comments from the discipline and inspection bodies, as well as other materials that reflect the result of the cadre investigation. The investigation documents and files should be built and managed by the organization and personnel departments in accordance with its authority in cadre management.

4 Decision through discussion

Decision through discussion is the process by which party committees at all levels make decisions on the appointment of cadres in accordance with the authorities of cadre management. The *Regulation on the Selection and Appointment of Leading Cadres* makes a clear stipulation about the selection and appointment of cadres in aspects such as the people who make appointments, the candidates, procedures and requirements.

(1) Brewing process before the decision

Candidates to be appointed for leadership posts should be subject to the brewing process with the participation of relevant leading members of party organizations (groups), standing committees, governments, Chinese People's Political Consultative Conferences (CPPCC), etc. before a decision is made, or that through discussion or on their appointment, is submitted to people's congresses. As for candidates to be appointed as leading members of internal institutions or departments, the opinions of leading members in charge at the upper level need to be solicited. This process is known as 'brewing'.

The brewing process actually exists throughout the whole process and in all aspects. It is vital link where democracy is promoted and consensus is achieved for the selection and employment of cadres, an efficient aspect of the implementation of democratic centralism and an important mechanism for deepening the understanding of cadres. The brewing process has played an important role in quickening the flow of information, soliciting opinions, attaining consensus, selecting the right person and making the most of him/her, and promoting solidarity among leading bodies.

(2) The process of and requirements for the decision through discussion

Meetings of party committees at all levels are convened for group discussion about the appointment and removal of cadres within the authority of cadre management.

In actual work, party committees hold a group discussion to decide on the appointment or removal of cadres that are within the jurisdiction of committees, or on the opinions they should propose about the recommendation and nomination of candidates for people's congresses; as for cadres within the jurisdiction of party committees at the upper level, party committees at the same level can also propose opinions on the appointment of cadres on secondment, the appointment of cadres related to the promotion and adjustment of positions within party committees should be proposed and submitted to party committees at the upper level according to the authorities of cadre management to be decided by them.

When party committees hold discussions on the decision to appoint and remove cadres, at least two thirds of members should be present and sufficient time should be allowed to understand the specifics and express their opinions freely. They should voice their agreement, disagreement or propose a delay in decisions relating to appointment and removal matters. Based on a full discussion, decisions are taken by oral vote, vote by raising hands or anonymous vote.

> **Column 4-2: Recommendation, nomination and democratic consultation in accordance with the law**
>
> *When the term of leading government bodies expires, local party committees need to recommend candidates for leadership posts to people's congresses or standing committees for the selection, appointment and confirmation of the appointment. Party committees are responsible for recommending and nominating candidates for leadership posts, and conducting democratic consultation in law process of election at the expiration of office terms in accordance with the law; this constitutes an important embodiment of the principle of ruling the party by the party, and an important guarantee for the party to manage state affairs. The process of conducting recommendation, nomination and democratic consultation is one that develops socialistic democratic politics and builds socialistic political civilization; it is also a process that makes an organic unity of adhering to the party's leadership and developing democracy fully, and is an act in strict accordance with the law.*
>
> *Recommendation refers to the process that local party committees, in accordance with the related stipulations of the Electoral Law of the NPC and the Organizational Law of Local People's Congresses at Various Levels and related requirements of recommendation of leading cadres to national organs by local party committees, recommend leading cadre candidates to people's congresses at the same level for appointment or to standing committees of people's congresses at the same level for the appointment and confirmation of the appointment.*
>
> *Nomination in accordance with the law refers to the process whereby, in accordance with related stipulations of the Organizational Law of Local People's Congresses at Various Levels, local party committees submit their nomination of candidates to governments for appointment after they make a decision through a discussion on leadership post candidates for government departments and institutions that don't need to go through selection, appointment and decision-making.*

Chapter 4

Candidates to be appointed and recommended candidates for principal positions of the leading body of local party committees and governments should generally go through the process of nomination by standing committees at the upper level and anonymous ballot vote by party national committees; when a meeting is not convened, decisions on urgent appointments are made by standing committees after soliciting the opinions of all members of party national committees.

Formation of the 'two committees'

(1) Deciding on the candidacy (727 candidates)

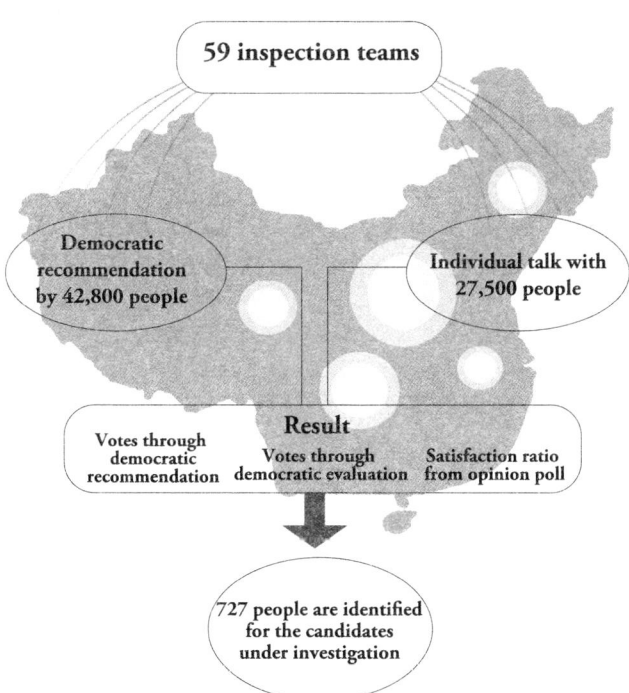

Graphic 4-2 The election of top leaders and leading organizations of the Central Committee of the CPC (1)

61

Leadership Selection and Appointment in China

(2) Candidates for preselection (532 persons)

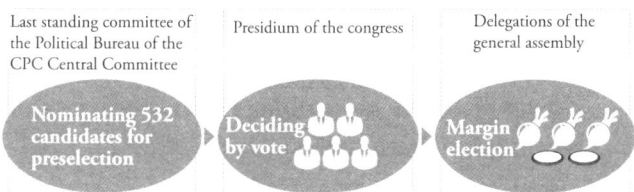

(3) Formal election (506 people)

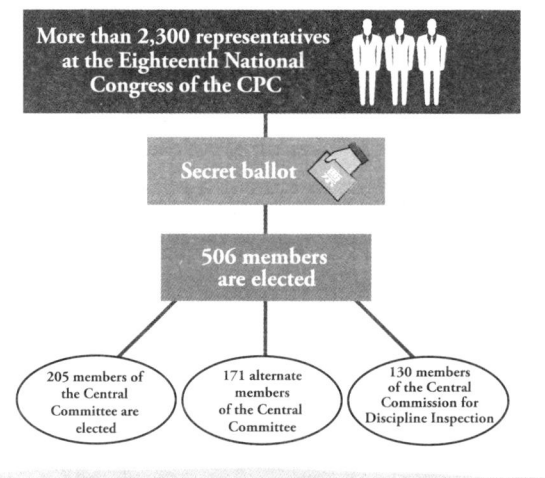

2. The formation of the Standing Committee of the Central Political Bureau and the Standing Committee of the Central Political Bureau

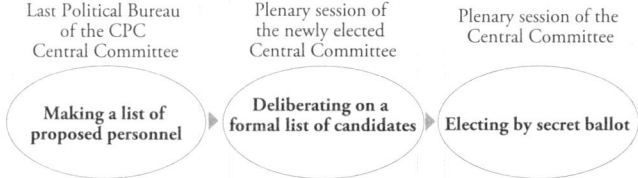

Total membership of the eighteenth central political bureau consists of:

25 committee members	7 standing committee members

Graphic 4-3 The election of top leaders and leading organizations of the Central Committee of the CPC (2)

Chapter 4

Tip: *Structural Diagram of the CPC Central Committee*

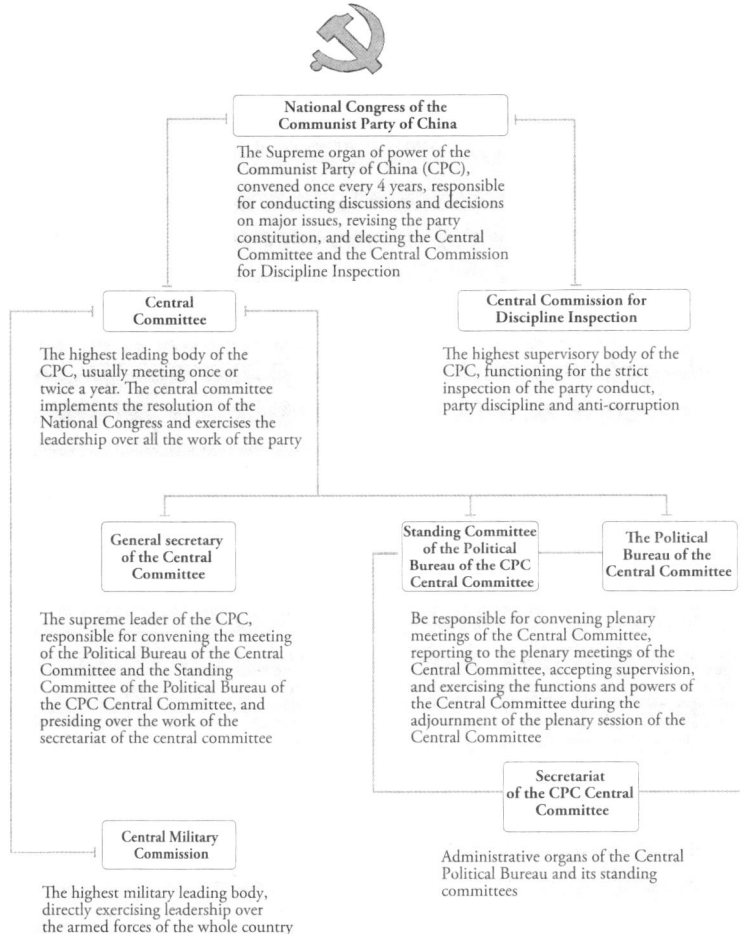

Graphic 4-4 The election of top leaders and leading organizations of the Central Committee of the CPC (3)

5 Appointment

Appointment refers to the process that organs in charge of the appointment and removal of cadres appoint leading cadres in accordance with the authorities of cadre management and regulations and procedures. The appointment is an important link in the selection and appointment of cadres, and an indispensable measure for cadres to start work officially after party committees (groups) have made the appointment decision.

63

The appointment of cadres is generally followed by a written notice of appointment and is usually publicized in the form of a document of appointment. Unlike in other countries, the appointment, as the last link in the selection and appointment of cadres, is a process that the supervision and management of cadres to be promoted is conducted in China. In accordance with the *Regulations for the Selection and Appointment of Leading Cadres of the Party and Governments*, the pre-service publicity system, the probation system and the on-the-job discussion system are adopted for the selection and appointment of cadres.

(1) Implementation of the pre-service publicity system

According to the regulations of the pre-service publicity system, the appointment of cadres for leadership positions below bureau level must be publicized before the issue of the notice of appointment after the decision based on the discussion of party committees (groups). The contents of the publicity should be credible and correct so that it can be used as the basis for investigation. A detailed explanation should be made if an exceptional promotion is involved. The publicity period should be no less than five working days. If there is little disagreement about the appointment, the procedures will be executed.

The implementation of the pre-service publicity system for the appointment of leading cadres of the party and government before their appointment is an institutional innovation that reflects a trend towards the expansion of democracy in cadre work, an organic combination of adhering to the principle of ruling cadres by the party and giving full play to democracy, an efficient means by which selection and appointment is strictly supervised with the help of the public, and an important measure to determine whether cadres win public recognition is examined. The appointment of leading cadres for important posts that need to be publicized is usually publicized in the form of a notice in news media such as newspapers, television, radio and the internet; the appointment of ordinary cadres needs to be publicized within the departments and institutions, usually in the form of issuing a publicity notice, making a conference announcement and posting a notice. Whatever form it adopts, the contents of the publicity must be known to the public and the conditions must be created for extensive participation.

(2) Implementation of the pre-service discussion system

According to the stipulations of the pre-service discussion system, party organizations need to be responsible for designating specially-assigned persons to talk to candidates to be appointed, point out their achievements and shortcomings, and propose requirements and issues worth attention. The on-the-job discussion, generally held after the official appointment, is usually conducted by the responsible people of the party committee, those in charge of the selection and appointment of cadres or the responsible people of the organization personnel department. In the on-the-job discussion, these responsible people should identify shortcomings, propose matters worth attention and put forward all the requirements of strict cadre management to newly appointed cadres.

Like the pre-service discussion system, the on-the-job discussion system is an important measure for strengthening the supervision and management of the appointment of cadres, playing an important role in examining whether cadres correctly perform their duties and strictly observe party rules and discipline in their positions. This system is not only a key link that has been formed for the procedures of selection and appointment in summing up the experience of cadre work over a long period, but also an efficient measure for giving full play to the party's ideological and political work and strengthening the education of cadres. The main task of talking to cadres is to outline the expectations required of them, making them aware of their responsibilities and duties, and the need to work hard in their new position. This will play an important role in guaranteeing the smooth appointment of cadres, realizing the normal transfer of work, and being especially helpful for the healthy growth and development of cadres.

(3) Implementation of the probation period system

The probation period system for the promotion and appointment of cadres for leadership posts below bureau level through non-election is one year. When the probation period expires, an assessment of procedures will be implemented. If a cadre proves competent, he will be officially appointed; otherwise, he will be removed and a new position will be arranged at the same rank of his previous position. The probation period system is both an extensive inspection of a cadre's competence to perform his duties and an efficient measure for the strict administration of cadres.

A newly appointed cadre can be counted as officially appointed only after he proves competent in the assessment at the end of the probation period. In this sense, the probation period system is part of the supervision and management process of the appointment, helpful for cadres to enhance the sense of responsibility and self-discipline and for them to experience the strict administration of party organizations in their new leadership posts. According to the stipulations of the probation period system, cadres will be removed from their posts on probation if they are involved in corruption or prove incompetent in the assessment at the end of the probation period. This system has further strengthened the supervision and management of cadres.

Chapter 5

Strict Administration of the Selection and Appointment of Cadres

Special emphasis has been placed on the principle of the supervision of cadres by the party in the selection and appointment of cadres. Specifically, the selection and appointment of cadres is in the charge of party organizations at all levels (party committees and their subordinate organizations at all levels). Since the 18th National Congress, in an attempt to strengthen the leadership and scrutiny of the selection and appointment of cadres by party organizations, the Central Committee of the CPC has formulated a series of management systems to exert strict supervision over the procedures of selection and appointment and elected leading cadres of the party and government, confining the exercise of power within an institutional framework. These systems are among the most stringent among political parties across the world.

1 Strict selection before appointment

On January 25, 2014, *Suggestions on Strengthening the Supervision of the Work of Selecting and Appointing Cadres* was promulgated. It stipulated that strict control should be exercised to ensure probity and resolutely prevent the promotion of cadres with corruption problems in the work of selection and appointment. Strict inspections should be made regarding a candidate's honesty and integrity. Suggestions from discipline inspection and supervision bodies must be collected and heard. Cadres with potential problems should not be submitted to party committees (groups) for discussion on possible appointment. If any candidate is reported on, careful inspections must be made. A strict audit of a cadre's archives must be conducted to clarify the candidate's identity, age, length of service, party standing, education background and experience, and no doubts should be overlooked. Careful investigation must be carried out if any problems are reported about the candidate during the publicity period. No promotion or appointment should be made before such problems are clarified.

To implement the *Suggestions*, from 2015 onward, the Organization Department of the CPC Central Committee launched a series of strict examinations and verification of cadres before their promotion. It includes auditing cadre files, verifying reports on personal matters and hearing opinions and suggestions from the discipline inspection and supervision bodies, and investigating reports on candidates on probation through specific clues mentioned in petition letters when promotion is involved. At the same time, the Organization Department has promulgated and implemented *Suggestions on Strengthening the Record of Cadre Selection and Appointment*. It stipulates that, should anyone suspected of corruption problems be promoted, an investigation of the process of selection and appointment must be carried out. These strict internal supervision measures have played an important role in ensuring the quality of the selection and appointment of cadres.

(1) Reviewing cadre files whenever promotion is involved

Cadre archives refer to the documents and materials that record information such as basic personal information, political ideology, professional ability, work performance and work achievements that serve as an important basis for the historical and comprehensive study of cadres.

The audit system of cadre archives before appointment began in 2014. Before then, in order to gain more advantages in the selection and appointment of cadres, some cadres found a short cut to rapid promotion by altering information such as their age, party standing, number of years worked, education background and work experience. To ensure that strict administration and supervision of cadres are fully implemented, the Central Organization Department lists the remediation of archive fraud issues as one of the six key tasks of rectifying malpractice in the selection and appointment of cadres. From October 2014, the audit work of personal archives of cadres has been carried out in three batches across the country. Since this date, the Central Organization Department has been regulating the strict audit of archives of those cadres to be selected, appointed and exchanged, along with demobilized military cadres and newly appointed cadres. The archives of cadres who are to be promoted must be audited so as to make sure that cadres with problems (usually, serious problems related to qualifications, capabilities and moral qualities) are prevented from being selected and appointed. In the second half of 2014 alone, the archives of more than 11,400 cadres under the direct management of provincial governments were audited before appointment. Out of this total, the appointment procedures of 111 cadres were terminated because of problems detected in their archives.

To carry out a special audit of personnel files of cadres nationwide and check cadre archives before appointment is a reflection of the strict administration of cadres and an important link of the stringent appointment standards and procedures that apply. The audit of cadre archives before appointment has become a routine aspect of the party's organization departments at all levels.

In the regulations for the selection and appointment of leading cadres, 'altering a cadre's archives or lying in areas such as identity, age, length of service, party standing, education background and experience' has been classified as one of the '10 nos'. Cadres who violate the above regulations will be warned within the party, and may even be expelled from the party with the reason recorded in their archives. According to relevant laws and regulations in China, should anyone be found altering or forging his archives, directly responsible persons in charge and other directly responsible personnel will be given administrative sanctions; if a crime is involved, they will be prosecuted for their criminal liability according to the law.

(2) Audit of the report on personal items in case of promotion

The implementation of the system for the report on personal items of leading cadres is an important measure for China in implementing the supervision and management of leading cadres. Since family property must be reported, report can be regarded as a property report system for cadres with Chinese characteristics. Taking into account the fact that leading cadres and the general public have the same privacy and property rights, the publicity of their personal property does not have a legal basis. Therefore, implementing the system for the report on personal items within the party is more in line with China's national conditions. This strict supervision measure is rarely found in other political parties across the world.

In May 2010, the General Office of the CPC Central Committee and the State Council revised and issued *Regulations on the Report on Personal Items of Leading Cadres*, requiring leading cadres at deputy county (department) level and above to report truthfully to organization departments on their personal matters covering 14 aspects such as marriage, overseas travel, income, real estate, investment, and occupation of their spouses and children, every year to comply with the supervision from party organizations. Since the issue of the regulations, organization and personnel departments at all levels arrange for leading cadres to complete the report on their personal matters at the beginning of each year.

In the early period of the implementation of the above regulations, since no networked data were supplied on personal matters such as personal property, real estate and investment, this information could not be verified. Some leading cadres paid little heed to the seriousness of filing a report on personal matters. They left out or wrongly supplied information to varying degrees while some even went so far as to deliberately alter or hide the truth.

Since the 18th National Congress of the CPC, the Central Committee adopted a series of major initiatives and put forward some strict requirements to strengthen the management and supervision of cadres. In the third plenary session of the 18th CPC Central Committee, the party made it clear that we should conscientiously implement the system of reports on personal matters for leading cadres, and carry out random checks to verify the work. To conscientiously implement the decision-making arrangements of the Central Committee, the Central Organization Department officially launched random checks to verify reports on the personal matters of leading cadres.

In January 2014, the Central Organization Department issued *Random Check Methods for the Verification of Personal Matters of Leading Cadres (Provisional)*. It defines clearly the principles, items, object scope, methods, results and disciplinary requirements for random checks. The focus of the verification is to compare the results that functional departments obtained with the contents provided by leading cadres themselves, so as to make sure that the information in the report is correct and credible. The work of verification, conducted in accordance with the administration authority of cadres by organization and personnel departments at all levels, is to be organized and put into practice by the cadre supervision institutions.

The random check comprises a random check and key spot check. The random check is carried out annually on a certain proportion of cadres. The proportion was increased to 10% from 3-5% in 2016. That is to say, of all the leading cadres at vice county (department) level and above across the country, 10% are subject to annual random checks by relevant departments for the credibility of their reports on personal matters. In 2014 alone, the Organization Department of the Party Central Committee conducted random checks on 1,550 cadres under the direct management of the Central Committee and leading cadre reserves at the provincial level, while all localities and departments conducted random checks on a total of 60,170 leading cadres at bureau and county level. This data is increasing every year. The key spot check refers to the verification of cadres to be promoted, candidates in the cadre reserve, targeted cadres in the work of inspection patrol and those involved in public tip-offs, based on the needs of the work.

In addition to the routine verification of the report on personal matters, the Central Organization Department started to implement a stricter supervision measure for the selection and appointment of cadres in 2015. Specifically, the candidates' report on related personal matters must be subject to overall verification before their appointment. It is what is known as 'verification before promotion'. In all cases involving the promotion and appointment of leading cadres, organization and personnel departments must verify the credibility of their reports on personal matters.

Column 5-1: Strict verification of the report on personal matters of candidates to be promoted in Shanghai

Since 2008, Shanghai has taken the lead in exploring and implementing the special declaration and audit system for major personal matters of leading cadres under the direct management of municipal governments, laying the foundation for carrying out random checks and verification. Since July 2013, Shanghai has consolidated and improved the assessment criteria and mechanism for random checks and verification. Since 2014, according to The Measures for Random Checks and Verification of the Report on Relevant Personal Matters of Leading Cadres (Provisional) issued by the Central Organization Department, leading cadres under the direct management of the municipal government to be promoted have been subject to 'verification before promotion', an all-round verification of their reports on relevant personal matters. We have conducted a targeted verification of the reports of candidates for leadership posts under the direct management of municipal governments on personal matters such as marriage, overseas travel, property, investment, and occupation of their spouses and children. Some leading cadres have been denied promotion because of dishonest declarations on personal matters in their reports.

In 2014, a total of 2,369 leading cadres at above deputy level went through verification in Shanghai. Among them, 1,809 cadres at the municipal bureau and department level were subject to random checks. A total of 560 cadres due to be promoted under the direct management of the municipal government and the leading body of municipal inspection units went through key spot checks. To guarantee an orderly and efficient operation of random inspection and verification, a contact work system involving 13 functional departments such as Bureau of Public Security, Bureau of Civil Administration, Bureau of Industry and Commerce, Bureau of Housing Management, Bureau of Human Resources and Social Services and the Securities Regulatory Commission, under the leadership of the Municipal Organization Department, have been subject to random inspection and verification, at the request of the Central Organization Department. They have also joined hands to form an information inquiry mechanism based on the separate responsibility and close cooperation of organization and personnel departments and relevant functional departments to ensure the stable and smooth progress of the verification.

Carrying out random checks and verification helps prevent the promotion and appointment of cadres with problems. Currently, Shanghai ensures that cadres due to be promoted under the direct management of the municipal government are subject to 'verification before promotion'. In 2014, a total of 345 cadres went through random inspection and verification and the promotion and appointment of two of them was delayed on account of dishonesty, omission or concealment in their reports on personal matters. In the random inspection, the relevant party committee discovered one cadre at deputy level who failed to declare a matter and they then decided to annul his party post. Random inspection and verification has also promoted the probity and self-discipline of leading cadres.

Leading cadres must regard it as a political and organizational discipline to report truthfully to their party organizations on relevant personal matters. Organization departments require that, should anyone fail to properly complete or intend to alter or omit information in the form, he must do it again or make a supplementary report within a definite time period, and the procedures for selection will be prolonged. If any leading cadre is caught failing to file the report truthfully, he must make an explanation. Based on the explanation, the cadre supervision and selection institution of the organization personnel department will decide if this cadre should be appointed or the procedures of selection be terminated; should anyone be caught deliberately concealing true information, he must not be promoted or appointed, or listed among the cadre reserve; should anyone get caught violating regulations, he must be ordered to amend within the definite time period; if anyone is suspected to be violating disciplines or laws, evidence must be submitted to the discipline inspection and supervision body for investigation and handling, ensuring the authority of the report system and the seriousness of the report discipline.

(3) Considering the advice of discipline inspection and supervision bodies 'before promotion'

China's discipline inspection and supervision bodies as special institutions for party members and national public servants to conduct supervision and inspection have the right to supervise, inspect, investigate and punish party members and public servants who violate party discipline and national laws.

Article 31 in *Regulations on the Selection and Appointment of Leading Cadres* clearly stipulates that the advice from the discipline inspection and supervision body where the candidate is affiliated should be considered when the inspection of his appointment is under way. The advice from inspection patrol institutions and other relevant departments can be taken into account when needed. The organization and personnel departments should take the advice from the discipline supervision and inspection institution about the candidate's party work style and construction of clean government.

Considering the advice of discipline inspection and supervision bodies 'before promotion' means strengthening the examination and verification of the cadres' honesty of administration before appointment, strictly examining and verifying the party work style and construction of clean government, making consideration of the advice from discipline inspection and supervision bodies an essential procedure of selection and appointment. Specifically, organization and personnel departments in charge of the selection and appointment of cadres should send on their own initiative the feedback form to discipline inspection and supervision bodies to solicit the real situation of whether cadres to be promoted and appointed violate party discipline and administrative regulations. If they are reported to have problems and these problems that should be verified are not being verified, their promotion and appointment must not be submitted to party committees (groups) for the decision and the appointment procedure must be terminated. If the reported problems are not in violation of party discipline, a strict observance of the standard must also be applied and the promotion and appointment must be suspended. In 2014 alone, the CPC Shanghai Municipal Commission for Discipline Inspection completed 78 solicitations of advice about 320 people upon the request of the Organization Department of the Municipal Party

Committee, offering advice such as the suspended appointment of cadres with problems.

The adoption of the supervision measure of soliciting advice before promotion is mainly to prevent the failure of a smooth flow of information between departments that select and appoint cadres and discipline inspection and supervision organs. Cadres have been taken away and put under investigation by discipline inspection and supervision bodies shortly after their appointment are declared by organization departments. This is because the selection and appointment of cadres and the discipline inspection and supervision operate in parallel with one other and have their separate work procedures and confidential disciplines.

(4) Investigation before promotion when a tip-off in the petition letter is involved

The pre-service publicity system has been adopted in the selection and appointment of cadres in China. Before the official appointment of cadres, organization departments must publicize the position and personal information of cadres to be promoted. For instance, if different opinions have been formed about cadres to be promoted or if they are thought unsuitable for the position or have problems in violation of discipline, any party member or cadre can report to party committees at the upper level and the discipline inspection commission through a special channel. If there are letters reporting that a cadre is suspected of committing dishonesty in administration or violating discipline during or before the pre-service publicity period, the organization department must suspend the appointment before verifying him.

This regulation also comes from *Suggestions on Strengthening Supervision over the Selection and Appointment of Cadres* promulgated and implemented in 2014. It clearly stipulates that the reported problems about cadres during the period of publicity of their appointment must be carefully investigated and verified by the provisions and the appointment must not be effected before verification. For example, the CPC Shanghai Municipal Committee implements very strict controls, requiring that discipline inspection and supervision departments and cadre supervision departments implement the examination and verification of reported problems in work style about cadres to be promoted and appointed during the period of the publicity of their appointment; if these problems can't be verified immediately and if significant doubt persists, advice such as cautious appointment, suspended appointment or inappropriate appointment must be given clearly.

Column 5-2: Discipline inspection and supervision bodies in China

As a collective name for discipline inspection bodies and national administrative supervision bodies, the discipline inspection and supervision body is an important component of China's political system. It is a complete organizational system ranging from the central government to local authorities, offering a reliable organizational guarantee for inspection and supervision and the implementation of discipline work.

The party's discipline inspection bodies mainly refer to party discipline inspection committees at all levels. They are special bodies responsible for implementing inner-party supervision, safeguarding the implementation of the party line, principles and policies, maintaining and implementing party discipline, and assisting party committees to build a clean government. The administrative supervision body is the supervisory body of the state supervision department and its subordinate department, responsible for supervising the state administrative body, state civil servants and other personnel appointed by state administrative bodies. The supervisory body of the State Council is in charge of supervision work of the whole country. The authorities of discipline inspection and supervision bodies refer to the rights for discipline inspection and supervision entrusted with by the party constitution, party regulations, national legislation, and the scope and limits for excising the rights.

The authority of the party's discipline inspection bodies mainly comprises the rights to supervise, inspect, investigate, advise and mete out disciplinary punishment. The right to supervise refers to the right of the discipline inspection organs to exercise supervision over party committees at their same level and their members, party committees at a lower level and their members within the scope of the jurisdiction of the constitution. The right to inspect refers to the right of discipline inspection bodies to exercise inspection over inspected subjects before, during and after the inspection, in accordance with the party constitution and other party regulations. The right to investigate refers to the right of discipline inspection bodies to conduct a preliminary verification of the violation of the discipline committed by party group members or party members in the report, charge and inspection, or the right to investigate and collect evidence when it is necessary to mete out disciplinary punishment and decide to put the case on file for the violation of party discipline of party group members or party members discovered in the preliminary verification. The right to advise refers to the right of discipline inspection bodies to give advice to departments where the inspected subjects belong, and to authorities at a higher level and other authorities that have the right to take charge, about how to handle the violation of party discipline they have already investigated. The right to mete out disciplinary punishment refers to the right of discipline inspection bodies to mete out disciplinary punishment to the inspected subjects in light of the nature of the violation of discipline and the seriousness of the case. The authorities of national administrative inspection bodies include the rights to inspect, investigate, advise and make decisions.

Since 1993, the Discipline Inspection Commission of the CPC at all levels and Administrative Supervision Bureaus at all levels have been merged to form a team of two departments, fulfilling two functions: discipline inspection and supervision.

2 Strict check upon appointment

In addition to the strict check before appointment, other important measures must be strictly adopted before the final appointment. These include the pre-service publicity system, pre-service informative and commitment system, pre-service discussion system and the probation system.

(1) Pre-service publicity system

Article 41 in *Regulations on the Selection and Appointment of Leading Cadres of the Party and Government* stipulates that the pre-service publicity system must be observed in the selection and appointment of leading cadres of the party and government. Specifically, when a cadre is promoted to a bureau-level leadership position, he must be subject to pre-service publicity within a certain scope after the party committee (group) has made a decision and are about to issue a notice of appointment unless he has been appointed to a special post or has already been publicized in the inspection of the election at the expiration of the office term. The contents of the publicity should be credible and correct for supervision. If it is an unconventional promotion, there should be an explanation. The period of publicity should be no less than five working days. If there is no objection about the publicized results when the period of publicity expires, the procedures for the appointment will be enacted.

Pre-service publicity about leading cadres at bureau level or leading cadres for important positions at county level are usually done through the form of media (newspapers, radio, television, the internet), while pre-service publicity about cadres at county level within internal bodies and other non-leadership cadres is carried out in the form of a notice within the institution where they work. The contents of the publicity include the cadre's name, gender, party attachment, birth date, current position resume and new position. In some localities, the work performance, previous positions and personal family situation are included in the publicity.

The period of the publicity, starting from the second day of publication of the notice, should last no fewer than five business days, not including festivals and holidays.

The pre-service publicity system is not only a democratic procedure for selecting and appointing cadres, but also an important way to effectively supervise the process. Corresponding to 'pre-service verification' when a tip-off in the form of petition letter is involved, the pre-service publicity system serves as a final hurdle to be cleared in the appointment. Even if a cadre has entered the procedure for appointment, the procedure can still be suspended or postponed until the reported problems are cleared up if real-name or anonymous tip-offs are involved.

(2) Pre-service notification and the commitment system

In order to better fulfill its inspection responsibilities of newly appointed cadres, some local party organizations issue them with a notification of pre-service responsibilities, notifying them of the duties, responsibilities, regulations and discipline in written form, and demanding that they sign up to declare commitment.

At present, the pre-service notification and commitment system is not universally implemented. But this system is a practical way of reminding cadres of their responsibilities and supervising them. In fact, many cadres don't have a comprehensive understanding of the regulations for the strict administration of cadres and the specifics of party discipline regulations. The pre-service notification and commitment system notifies newly appointed cadres of the regulations and discipline that should be strictly observed, sets up supervision at the very beginning of the appointment and is helpful in reminding them to fulfill the responsibilities commensurate with their position and strictly follow party rules and discipline. Just like the oath of office, it also allows newly appointed cadres to make a solemn promise.

(3) Conversation system after appointment

Article 43 of the *Regulations on the Selection and Appointment of Leading Cadres of the Party and Government* stipulates that the conversation system after appointment must be introduced in the selection and appointment of leading cadres. Specifically, the party organization designates someone to have a talk with newly appointed cadres, affirm their achievements, point out shortcomings, make requirements and propose matters worth attention.

In the previous *Regulations on the Selection and Appointment of Cadres of the Party and Government*, the conversation system after appointment involved just one procedure. But the new regulations elevate them to the position of a special system. Like the conversation system after appointment, the conservation is also an important measure for strengthening the management of the selection and appointment of cadres, playing an important role in ensuring that newly appointed cadres properly perform their work duties and strictly abide by party discipline in their new positions.

The pre-service discussion is usually arranged after the official appointment. It is normally conducted by the responsible person of the party committee, the responsible person in charge of the selection and appointment of cadres and the responsible person of the organization and personnel department. Newly appointed cadres should be notified of their shortcomings and weak points, any particular concerns and all the specific requirements for the strict administration of cadres.

(4) Probation system

Article 42 of *Regulations on the Selection and Appointment of Leading Cadres of the Party and Government* stipulates that the probation system must be adopted in the appointment of leading cadres of the party and government. It requires a probation period for the promotion of non-elected cadres below bureau level of one year. When the probation period expires, they must meet the assessment procedures. If they prove unequal to the demands of the position, they should be demoted to a position in their previous rank.

The probation period system is not only an extensive inspection of the ability of cadres to perform their duties but also an effective measure for the strict administration of cadres. According to the stipulations of the probation period system, cadres must be removed from their positions if they have corruption problems or fail to pass the assessment at the end of probation. This system has further strengthened the supervision and management of the appointment of cadres. A newly appointed cadre could only be officially appointed if he passes the assessment. In this sense, the probation period is an inspection and management in the process of the appointment, helpful for cadres to enhance their sense of responsibility and self-discipline, and undergo strict administration from the very beginning of their new leadership positions.

3 Strict management after appointment

Having passed through the many appointment procedures, a cadre takes his leadership position. But this is just the beginning, for he has to face strict constraints and supervision from a variety of party rules and discipline. Since the 18th National Congress of the CPC, an all-out effort to enforce strict party discipline has become an important strategic policy of the CPC Central Committee. A very basic element of an all-out effort to enforce strict party discipline is to run the party strictly. It could be said that such strict running of the party is unprecedented, and such strictness is also rare among political parties across the world.

In addition to the regular annual report on relevant personal matters, the Central Organization Department has promulgated and implemented a series of relevant regulations for strict cadre management since the 18th National Congress of the CPC. In addition to a positive incentive system for selection and appointment, regulations requiring cadres to be ready to work at both higher and lower levels have been introduced. In one term of service after another, the strict cadre management runs from beginning to end.

- Leading cadres are prohibited from participating in expensive social training.
- Leading cadres are prohibited from holding concurrent salaried posts in enterprises and associations.
- Leading cadres are prohibited from permitting their spouses and relatives to go into business.
- The system to demote leading cadres to a lower rank if they fail to perform their duties.

(1) Leading cadres are not allowed to participate in expensive social training

In 2014, the Central Organization Department and the Ministry of Education jointly issued *Notice on Matters Concerning the Strict Regulation of the Participation of Leading Cadres in Social Training*, prohibiting leading cadres from using education funds of their departments to participate in expensive social training.

Education and training for cadres in China has received more intense attention and higher input than for other political parties across the world. However, the Central Organization Department has strict system requirements for the participation of cadres in education and training. In 2014, *Regulations on the Training and Education of Cadres* was revised and then officially promulgated and implemented. Each leading cadre of the party and government above county level must participate in all sorts of pre-job training, professional training and other special training held by organization and personnel departments. In addition to party schools and cadre academies affiliated to organization departments at all levels, other social training institutions (institutions of higher learning or training consultancy firms) are also allowed to hold training projects for the education of cadres. However, cadres are banned by official order to use education and training funds to participate in training projects that charge substantially.

The Notice stipulates that leading cadres are prohibited from participating in the training courses that charge high fees and various types of service in the name of learning. Those who have already participated in these activities must withdraw immediately; if leading cadres have taken part in social training that doesn't charge high fees, the charge should be borne by themselves instead of being reimbursed by their departments or subsidized by any institution or other person in whatever form.

Leading cadres are prohibited from using education funds of their departments to participate in all sorts of social training that charge substantial sums. This is an important institutional regulation for the strict administration of cadres. Before the promulgation and implementation of the notice, the participation of leading cadres in training projects of institutions of higher learning and social training institutions such as EMBAs, post-EMBAs, and senior leadership seminars and workshops were funded by their departments, causing the embezzlement and abuse of public resources to a certain extent. The regulation of the participation of leading cadres in social training is an important measure for strengthening clean governance. The key to reduce the possibility of being corrupted is to make leading cadres scrupulous in separating public from private interests and deprive them of their privileges.

(2) Leading cadres are prohibited from taking salaried positions in enterprises and associations

In developed countries in Europe and the US, the phenomenon of government officials seeking employment in private institutions after they resign or retire is called a 'revolving door' by the public. The 're-employment' of resigned or retired officials has always been the focus of a legal society. All countries have drafted laws and regulations to carry out institutional constraint of this phenomenon. Usually, they set up a 'frozen period' of between one and two years, during which resigned or retired officials are prohibited from taking up jobs that are related to the responsibilities in their previous positions, on behalf of themselves, enterprises or institutions.

China has adopted stricter management of the re-employment of resigned or retired officials. As early as 2004, the CPC Central Committee made clear stipulations for taking concurrent positions in enterprises of leading cadres of the party and government. In 2013, the CPC Central Committee Organization Department promulgated and implemented *Suggestions for Further Regulating Leading Cadres of the Party and Government to Take Part-time Jobs in Enterprises*, which requires that the circumstances of resigned or retired leading cadres taking part-time jobs or obtaining employment in enterprises should be put under strict check. A strict examination and approval process over the rights and powers of cadre managers is still needed for positions in enterprises where the experience of cadres is in particularly high demand. The relevant specific stipulations are divided into three kinds of situations.

- Within three years of resigning or retirement, leading cadres are prohibited from obtaining employment in enterprises within their scope of business and in regions within the jurisdiction of their previous positions. Nor are they allowed to engage in profit-making activities that are related to the business areas they used to work in their previous positions.

- Within three years of resignation or retirement, leading cadres must report in advance to party organizations of institutions where they worked previously if they plan to obtain employment in enterprises outside the scope of business of, and in regions outside, the jurisdiction of their previous position; only after the party organizations of the institutions where they worked previously conduct an examination and verification in accordance with relevant regulations and gain the approval of organization and personnel departments at a correspondingly higher level, can they take a part-time job or obtain reemployment.

– Within three years of resignation or retirement, leading cadres should report to party organizations of institutions where they worked previously for organizations of party committees to conduct an examination and verification in accordance with relevant regulations and present to the corresponding organization and personnel departments to be put on record according to the authorities of cadre management, whether they obtain employment in enterprises within the scope of the business of, and in regions within the jurisdiction of, their previous positions, or outside the scope of business of, and in regions outside the jurisdiction of, their previous positions.

– After resignation or retirement, a leading cadre of the party and organization still enjoys the retirement benefits of a state public official, as well as the identity of state public servant. Although he could be allowed to take a part-time job in an enterprise with approval, he is prohibited from gaining payment in forms such as a salary, bonus or allowance, or seeking equity and other additional benefits, and nor could he take more than one part-time job. He is also not allowed to serve two consecutive terms of the position he holds. If his part-time job complies with the tenure system, then his reappointment, which should not exceed two terms, must be subject to examination and approval and put to record when the first term expires. The age limit for part-time job positions is 70.

The employment of leading cadres of the party and government in enterprises is not only limited to leadership posts but also to honorary posts such as consultant and posts such as external director, independent director and independent supervisor, be they part-time or full-time jobs. These regulations indicate that state public officials are prohibited from taking advantage of their positions to seek benefits for enterprises, companies or private institutions, thereby obtaining additional benefits for themselves. To quote a popular catch-phrase: "You either stay in your official post living plainly or seek employment in enterprises living comfortably."

Chapter 5

Sorting out the employment of leading cadres by Zhou Xiyue, Xinhua News Agency

In addition to the strict rules on leading cadres taking up part-time jobs in enterprises, cadre management departments also have clear requirements for the employment of leading cadres in social associations. As early as 2007, the State Council issued opinions requiring that civil servants still in service are prohibited from taking up leadership posts in industry associations. If their work demands it, their employment must be subject to strict examination and they must gain approval for the post in accordance with the regulations. In 2014, the Central Organization Department issued a document requiring that the re-employment of retired leading cadres in non-government organizations (including leadership positions, honorary positions and executive directors) must be examined and put on record. Once approval is obtained, they could take up a single position in a social group, and when the term expires and they want to serve a second term, they must go through a new round of examination and gain approval. Serving more two terms is prohibited and they must not be older than 70 years old.

In 2015, the Central Committee of the CPC revised the *Regulations on the Disciplinary Sanction of the CPC*. The regulations stipulate clearly that if the employment of leading cadres in economic entities or social organizations violates the above regulations or they get extra benefits such as a salary, bonus or allowance through such employment, they must be disciplined according the circumstances. If it is a minor violation, they must be given a warning or a serious warning; if it is a relatively serious violation, they must be deprived of their party posts or placed on probation; if it is a serious violation, they must be expelled from the party. When there is a re-employment violation of the above regulations involving resigned or retired leading cadres in enterprises and intermediary organizations in the same business area, or in regions within the jurisdiction of their previous positions, or if they engage in profit-making activities related to the business scope of their previous positions, disciplinary action must follow. If it is a relatively minor violation, they must be given a warning or a serious warning; if it is a relatively serious violation, they must be deprived of their party posts; if it is a serious violation, they must be placed on probation within the party.

It also stipulates that if resigned or retired leading cadres are re-employed in listed companies or fund management companies as independent directors, independent supervisors or the like and that this violates the above regulations, they must be disciplined. If it is a minor violation, they must be given a warning or a serious warning; if it is a relatively serious violation, they must be deprived of their party posts; if it is a relatively serious violation, they must be placed on probation within the party.

(3) Regulations on the engagement of spouses or relatives of leading cadres in trade and business

In addition to the strict regulation on leading cadres' engagement in business activities or their employment in enterprises, Chinese cadre management institutions have made a strict regulation on the engagement of spouses or relatives of leading cadres in trade and business. As early as 1985, the Central Committee of the CPC promulgated no fewer than 20 bans on the engagement of spouses or relatives of leading cadres in trade and business. In 2015, Shanghai municipal government issued *Regulations on Further Regulating the Engagement of Spouses or Relatives of Leading Cadres in Trade and Business (Provisional)*. It states:

- Spouses of leading cadres at Shanghai municipal level (equivalent to provincial and ministerial level) are prohibited from engaging in trade and business. The children and spouses of their children are prohibited from engaging in trade and business in Shanghai.

- For leading cadres at the principal level of all the parties and governments and the leading body of public security bodies, procuratorial authorities and judicial authorities that have relatively concentrated authority, their spouses are prohibited from engaging in trade and business, and their children and the spouses of their children are prohibited from engaging in trade and business within the business scope of, or in the regions within their jurisdiction, or engaging in trade and business that might cause conflicts with public interests in Shanghai.

- Apart from those leaders, the spouses, children and children's spouses of other leading cadres are prohibited from engaging in trade and business within the business scope of or in regions within their jurisdiction, or engaging in trade and business that might cause conflicts with public interests in Shanghai.

- 20% of leading cadres who haven't declared the engagement of their spouse, children and their children's spouses in trade and business will be subject to an annual random inspection. The objective is to discover any omissions or concealments. If any leading cadre is found to have violated the above regulation, he must either order his relatives to quit their business or resign himself from his post.

As to the practical significance of the above regulations, Ying Yong, deputy secretary of Shanghai Municipal Committee of the CPC, said that it is the inevitable requirement for the strict implementation of the strategy of ruling the party, and for the party to supervise and rule the party strictly. From the historical and international experience, it is necessary to regulate the engagement of cadres' relatives in trade and business. Many countries have made efforts in this regard. For instance, some regulations expressly stipulate that administrative officials are prohibited from taking advantage of their positions to prevail on others to solicit interests for themselves or their relatives, and limitations have been set for the engagement of cadres' relatives in some profit-making activities.

The common features of corruption are bribery and abuse of power. The engagement of leading cadres' relatives in trade and business can easily lead to a conspiracy of government officials and business, conduct of trading power with money and the transfer of illegitimate interests. The Central Committee of the CPC speaks highly of Shanghai for its efforts applying the above regulations on the engagement of leading cadres' spouses and children in trade and business. We believe that such measures will be implemented throughout the country in the near future.

(4) Mechanism for leading cadres to be downgraded if they fail to perform their duties

In 2015, the CPC made significant achievements in ruling the party strictly. In the same year, the CPC Central Committee issued *Regulations for Leading Cadres to be Ready to Accept a Higher or Lower Post (Provisional)*. Leading cadres will not only be held accountable and removed from power for their errors in work or violation of discipline, they may also be demoted or transferred to another position for neglect of duty or an inability to carry out their duty.

The regulations make a clear stipulation about the form, means and procedures for adjusting the positions of leading cadres who are incompetent at work. They not only require that cadres are severely disciplined for their serious violation of laws and discipline, but also that they are disciplined for their ignorance of the rules in politics, negligence of duty in work, lack of ability and impractical work style. It will surely have significant and far-reaching influence in improving the mechanism to make cadres ready to accept a higher or lower post, and in enhancing the vigor and vitality of all cadres.

For instance, the regulations include a list of cases where cadres are unfit for their present positions and need to be transferred to other positions (that is to say, demoted to a lower rank). They are: failing to strictly abide by the party's political discipline and political rules and firmly carry out the party's basic line and all kinds of policies; wavering in holding fast to the party's ideals and beliefs and in adhering to the major principles, or taking a noncommittal stand, or airing opinions not consistent with the party's line; disregarding the party's principle of democratic centralism, acting in a dictatorial, weak or slack manner, refusing to execute or change decisions made by party organizations, or causing interpersonal disputes in the leadership body; having a weak sense of organization, refusing to implement the system for reporting on important matters, or acting dishonestly or making concealments in filling in reports on personal matters; violating the Central Committee's requirements for clean governance or failing to observe related regulations on clean governance; being afraid or failing to take responsibility, developing a sloppy work style, or causing great annoyance among cadres and the public; failing to perform the duties or fulfill the tasks according to requirements, lagging behind in work, or causing relatively serious errors; causing adverse effects because of bad conduct, social morality, work ethics and family ethics; being rendered unfit for the position because their spouses, or their children, have emigrated abroad (or overseas regions).

Leading cadres of party organizations and government institutions at all levels must be ready to accept either a higher or lower post. They must be removed from leadership posts and be disciplined within party organizations if they fail to observe their duties conscientiously and competently without necessarily committing major errors or seriously violating discipline and laws; if they lack a strong sense of enterprise, a sense of responsibility and muddle along in their work; if they shirk responsibility when problems arise; and if they cause great damage to the cause of the party and the people because they deliberately ignore the discipline and laws by abusing power and trade it for personal gain. Only when better-performing cadres are kept in their position while those with inferior work performances are removed and demoted, can progressiveness and work competence be ensured for leading cadres at all levels. This has already been the trend in managing the appointment of cadres in China. In future, the management of leading cadres at all levels will be increasingly strict, and China's construction of a clean and honest government will surely enjoy an ever brighter and more hopeful future.

Chapter 6

Examination and Evaluation in the Selection and Appointment of Cadres

In the system of the selection and appointment of cadres of the party and governments in China, some cadres, such as newly appointed civil servants, are selected and appointed through examination and evaluation. The *Civil Law of the PRC* clearly stipulates that newly appointed civil servants should pass the national civil service exams. The public selection of some civil servants is also realized through evaluation and examination. Evaluation and examination is also frequently needed in the process of competitive selection for posts in internal bodies and public selection for leading cadres. In recent years, the Central Organization Department has introduced computerized assessment and psychological quality evaluations when selecting senior officials, thus making the selection and appointment of cadres more elaborate and scientific.

Special agencies have been set up for the examination and evaluation within organizations of party committees at all levels. These special agencies are responsible for the design of examination questions, the categorization of questions and the development of scientific test evaluation for the selection and appointment of cadres of the party and government. In the Department of National Human Resources and Social Security, there is also a personnel testing center with responsibility for specific technical work relating to national civil service recruitment examinations.

1 Admission by exam for new civil servants

The civil service examination system in China has a long history, growing gradually from immaturity to perfection. The current *Civil Servants Act* is the basis for civil service recruitment. It makes corresponding regulations for the principles, scope and specific requirements for the admission by exam for civil servants. This system applies to civil servant positions lower than those of chief staff member and other civil servants of non-leadership positions of the equivalent level who are to be recruited by agencies at all levels.[1] China's civil service system draws on the west's civil service system, changing 'admission by exam for national staff' to admission by exam for the national civil service'. Localities and departments at all levels have formulated and issued methods and rules for implementation, forming a system of regulations on admission by exam that covers many elements such as a written test, interview, physical examination, assessment and supervision. Work on the civil service examination system has been gradually regulated and institutionalized. The policies, plans, positions, qualifications, procedures and results of admission by exam are all publicized, so the process is also known as the 'glass house competition'. Since the National Ministry of Personnel (now the National Ministry of Human Resources and Social Security) promulgated *Interim Regulations on the Recruitment of National Civil Servants in 1993*, and since the national civil service exam was implemented in 1994, many talented individuals with an interest in administrative management have been introduced into the team of civil servants. They have played an important role in improving the quality of civil servants, and enhancing the vitality of state administrative bodies. Between 2003 and 2006, 330,000 civil servants were recruited across China. Among the newly recruited civil servants in central state bodies, the proportion of those who hold a bachelor's degree or above has been maintained above 99%.[2]

The civil service examination system is not restricted in terms of identity, location, residence, nationality, education and so on, thus having played a positive role in helping maintain social fairness and justice, and promoting the optimal flow of talent. In 2012, the number of applicants for the civil service in central offices totaled 155,000, of whom 82.3% were from ordinary families. In 2011, central offices and agencies directly under them hired more than 15,000 civil servants, 87.1% of whom came from ordinary families; in 2010, central offices and agencies directly under them hired more than 14,000 civil servants, 93.4% of whom came from ordinary families.[3] In ethnic minority areas, some favorable policies such as a lower admission

---

[1] *Regulations on Civil Servants Admission (Provisional)*, The Organization Department of the Central Committee of the CPC and Ministry of Personnel, issued on Novemember 6, 2007.
[2] *Admission of Civil Servants*, eds., Yang Shiqiu, Wang Jingqing, Beijing: China Personnel Press, Party Construction Readings Press, 2009
3 *More than 80% of Newly Hired Civil Servants Come from Ordinary Families*, Sheng Ruowei, Du Rong, People's Daily, March 2, 2012

levels have been implemented to hire civil servants, so that the proportion of ethnic minorities increased from 6.6% in 2010 to 7.3% in 2011, showing a clear upward trend.[4]

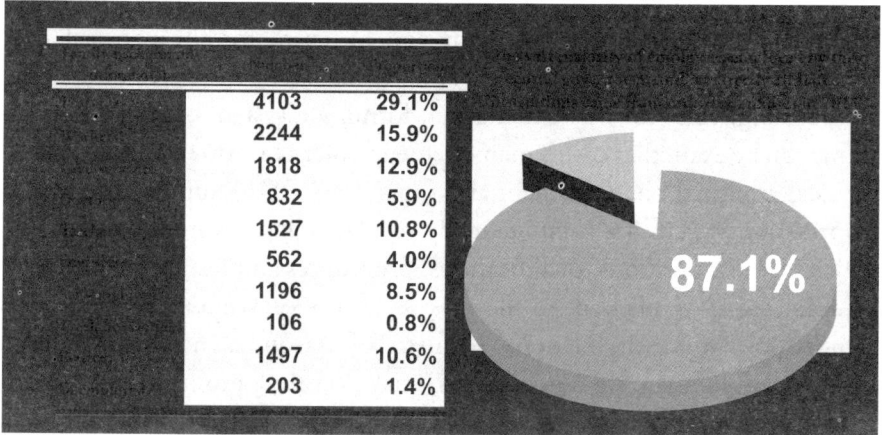

(1) Procedures for admission by exam for civil servants

The basic procedures for admission by exam for civil servants include preparation for admission, judgment on admission and the procedures for the recruitment of civil servants. The central civil service department is responsible for organizing the recruitment of civil servants for central offices and the agencies directly under them. Provincial civil service departments are responsible for organizing the recruitment of civil servants for local authorities at all levels and, when necessary, they may authorize subordinate municipal civil service departments to be responsible for it in its place.

1) Releasing the notice of the admission by exam for civil servants. State administrative agencies draw up the plan for the admission by exam for civil servants in terms of the number to be enrolled, professions, required qualifications and recruitment range based on actual needs. Then, each recruitment department delivers its recruitment plan to personnel departments of the government at the same level which in turn drafts a recruitment plan for the year after overall consideration. The recruitment plan will be revised and sent to the competent hiring authority and the plan will be put into practice after approval. Issuing the notice of admission by exam is the first step in publicizing the admission by exam for civil servants. It lists recruitment agencies, position vacancies, the required education

---

[4] *Grassroots Experience Carries More Weight in the Admission of Civil Servants for Central Offices*, Sheng Ruowei, People's Daily, October 11, 2011

level and work experience, the type of examination, examination subjects and so on. The notice is generally publicized through media outlets such as newspapers, radio and television.

2) Registration and qualification check. With the continuous development of network technology, the admission by exam for cadres of central state bodies and departments of all local authorities mainly take the form of online registration, so as to save the time and costs of the organizers and candidates. At the same time, the admission by exam authorities and employers conduct an eligibility review for applicants in order to decide who are qualified to take part in the examination.

3) The admission by exam for civil servants consists of written tests and oral interviews. There are two rounds of tests: in the first round, applicants take a written test; in the second round, those who have passed the first round participate in an interview. Written tests are generally held by civil service authorities, while interviews are conducted by national authority departments. The written examination for admission to central state bodies include an administrative aptitude test and essay writing. Those who apply for posts that demand the use of a non-common language or special professional background need to sit professional examinations.

Written test questions are designed in a unified way by the civil service authorities. Different score requirements are set for central, provincial, city (prefecture), county (district) and below county level. The required scores are lower for those who apply for positions in western regions and remote and poverty-stricken areas, and for those who are committed to be college-graduate village officials.

Following the release of written test results from low to high, a list of candidates qualified for interview and professional subjects is determined and publicized on a specially designated website. Interviews are organized by recruitment agencies and generally take the form of structured interviews or group discussions without the presence of leaders. Should the number of applicants who pass the required scores for the written test of public subjects fail to meet the right proportion for the planned number of enrollment, the shortfall must be made up by people who passed the exam but applied for posts in defferent departments. The interview evaluation panel are responsible for conducting an independent and objective evaluation concerning the performance of these candidates, and calculate the final results based on combining the scores for the written test and interview.

4) Admission by exam agencies determine the candidacy according to the test results, and conduct the qualification check for registration, investigation and physical examination. Investigation should focus on two aspects: political quality of the candidates and requirements for the posts. We usually adopt three assessment methods based on the review of files, discussions and seminars.

5) Admission by exam agencies draft and publicize the list of candidates suggested to be hired based on the results of the tests, investigation and physical examination.

6) When the publicity period is over, the agencies responsible for central admission by exam submit a list of candidates to be recruited to the central civil service authorities. Local admission by exam agencies at all levels submit a list to provincial civil service authorities or city civil service authorities divided into districts to be reviewed and approved.

7). Probation and training. Newly recruited civil servants should be put on a one-year probation. Qualified candidates will be hired while the unqualified will be dismissed once the probation period expires.

> **Special column: The heat and difficulty of the 'national examination'**
>
> In China, the admission by exam for the national civil service is the largest and the most extensive vocational qualification examination. It is also the only way for people to enter politics and serve the country, and is hence called the 'national examination'. Since the implementation of this examination, the number of applicants has been increasing every year. The chart below contains statistics about the number of applicants, the number recruited and the enrollment rate for this exam over the past 10 years. It shows that the number of applicants is very large, but the annual enrollment rate is less than 2% due to the limited number of positions. Therefore, it could also be said that the national civil service exam is the most difficult vocational qualification examination of its kind in the world.
>
> The number of applicants, number recruited and enrollment rate for the admission by exam for the national civil service, 2004 to 2014
>
> | Year | Number of applicants (m) | Number recruited | Enrollment rate |
> |---|---|---|---|
> | 2014 | 1.52 | 19,538 | 1.29% |
> | 2013 | 1.383 | 20,879 | 1.51% |

Year	Number of applicants (m)	Number recruited	Enrollment rate
2012	1.33	17,941	1.35%
2011	1.415	16,205	1.15%
2010	1.042	15,526	1.28%
2009	1.04	13,566	1.28%
2008	0.80	13,977	1.67%
2007	0.536	12,724	2.38%
2006	0.365	10,282	2.86%
2005	0.311	8,400	2.70%
2004	0.181	7,900	4.35%

Some figures obtained from the People's Daily website

(2) Main methods for the admission by exam of civil servants

The admission by exam for the national civil service comprises a written test on public subjects, interviews and a test on professional subjects. The written test on public subjects is made up of an administrative aptitude test and an essay. The interview includes a structured interview and group discussion without the presence of the leadership. Professional subjects mainly involve professional knowledge and skills such as the command of a foreign language or financial expertise specially required for a particular position. The written test is usually unified at the national or provincial level. The interview and the test on professional subjects are conducted by employers in accordance with the procedures and requirements.

1). Administrative aptitude test (AAT)

The AAT is a regulated test designed to measure the administrative aptitude of candidates, constituting an important part of the written test for the admission by exam for civil servants of central state bodies and other state bodies. The test includes five major elements: speech and expression, quantitative relationship, judging and reasoning, basic knowledge and analysis of materials. According to the annual syllabus requirements, there will be some changes in the form of the test and number of items tested.

The speech and expression test guages an applicant's ability to use language, to think and to communicate, and the power to grasp written material in a quick and accurate way. The targeted items are classified into: the ability to locate key information and important details based on the given reading material, the ability to correctly understand specific words and sentences of the material, the ability to generalize the main idea and central topic of the material, the ability to judge whether newly formed statements are consistent with the original meaning conveyed in the material, the ability to correctly infer the implied information through the context of the material, the ability to determine the author's attitude, intentions, tendencies and purpose, the ability to make the right choice of words, and so on. Common test items are reading comprehension and filling in blanks that focus on logic and expression.

The test of quantitative relationship evaluates an applicant's ability to understand the quantitative relationship between matters and resolve the problems caused by such a relationship. It mainly involves analyzing, inferring, judging and operating that are related to the given data. Common test items are numerical reasoning and mathematical operation.

Judging and inferring measure an applicant's ability to analyze and infer the relationship between different matters. It involves skills such as understanding, comparing, inducting and deducting graphics, word concepts, relationships between matters and written materials. Common test items include graphical reasoning, definition, analogical reasoning and logical reasoning.

Analysis of materials mainly measures an applicant's ability to conduct a comprehensive understanding, analyzing and processing materials such as various forms of text, graphics and other information. This part usually consists of statistical charts, numbers and text materials.

Basic knowledge measures the extent to which an applicant knows basic knowledge, and his ability to apply this basic knowledge to analyze and judge problems. It places emphasis on measuring the level of understanding, the integrated management of the basic quality of the conditions of society, involving fields such as politics, the economy, the legal system, history, culture, geography, environment, nature, science and technology.

The time limit for the administrative aptitude test is 120 minutes and the maximum point score is 100. The test involves a variety of types of elements and is organized in aspects such as the types of questions, the number of items and difficulty based on the purpose of the test and the quality of the applicants.

In the understanding of speech and expression, for example, applicants are required to use certain language knowledge to approach a given text and choose the best answer to the questions set for it.

For example: *In ancient times, whenever a war started, artisans would become the object of contention. Since artisans owned the most important technology, they representing the most advanced social productive forces. Today, in spite of the fact that modern science and technology has replaced manual skills, and has become the most powerful element of productivity, traditional artisanship can be enhanced with the help of modern science and technology, continuing to serve the public.*

This text is intended to illustrate which of the following:

A. *Traditional artisanship can develop effectively through its marriage with modern technology.*

B. *At any time, social productive force is the first element of social development.*

C. *Modern technological advances profoundly impact traditional handicrafts.*

D. *Modern technology can address the productivity constraints of traditional artisanry.*

(Answer: A. In the last sentence, we know 'traditional artisanship' is enhanced through 'modern technology'. It can be seen that traditional artisanship can develop through its marriage with modern technology. So, option 'A' is the right answer.)

2) Essay test

The essay is a test that measures the basic ability that one should have for work in the agencies. The test paper contains no multiple choice questions; instead, candidates are required to write detailed answers. The essay test is made up of two types of paper: one based on the requirements for the integrated management category at the provincial (including sub-provincial) level and the other integrated management and administrative law enforcement category at the city (prefecture) level and the level below it.

The essay for provincial (including sub-provincial) integrated management positions measures an applicant's capacity for reading comprehension, integrated analysis, raising and resolving problems, and writing skills.

The capacity for reading comprehension – requiring candidates to have a comprehensive grasp of the contents of the given materials, an accurate understanding of the meaning of the materials, a correct generalization of the ideas contained in the facts, and a close revelation of the fundamental question.

The capacity for synthesizing – requiring candidates to analyze, generalize concerning the whole or part of the contents, the ideas or questions of the given materials, and reflect on the given materials from different perspectives, so as to give a reasonable inference or evaluation.

The capacity for raising and solving problems – requiring that candidates, based on their working or personal experience, are able to discover and determine issues, assess or weigh them so as to come up with possible measures to solve them.

Writing capacity – requiring candidates to precisely, properly, concisely and fluently express certain ideas by the skilled use of the appointed language, and methods such as instruction, narration and argumentation.

Essay tests for the integrated management and administrative law enforcement category at city (prefecture) level and the level below it mainly measure an applicant's capacity to understand, implement, solve and express.

The capacity for reading comprehension – requiring candidates to understand the main contents of the given materials, grasp the relationship between various parts of the materials, and properly explain the point of viewpoints and facts involved in the materials.

The capacity to implement – requiring candidates to precisely grasp the goals of the work and the intent of the organization, follow the principle of administration according to the law, and to complete the tasks according to the objective factual circumstances in a timely and efficient manner.

The capacity for problem solving – requiring candidates to make a correct analysis to determine specific problems by the use of their own knowledge and experience, and come up with practical measures or approaches.

The capacity for speech and expression – requiring candidates to deftly use the appointed language to precisely and reasonably explain, state and interpret specific events and viewpoints.

The essay test is divided into a number of parts with a maximum score of 100. It has a different writing assignment to the test of English as a foreign language (TOEFL), laying equal stress on the capacity to grasp the materials and express certain ideas. Therefore, the essay is a more demanding test. It first provides a certain number of given materials (cases), and then requires candidates to tackle the various writing topics for each material. For example, the test provides four paragraphs of materials, and require candidates to complete the following writing assignment:

Examples: ***Questions for essay test***

(a) Please fill in the three separate blanks in the given material 1 with a sentence for each which makes the conclusion semantically logical (10 points). These three sentences of no more than 100 words in total should be accurate, inclusive and concise.

(b) Please say something about 'whether the use of new technologies can break through the barriers of social structure' based on the given material 2 (20 points). The writing should be clear, well-founded, inclusive and concise, and comprise no more than 250 words.

(c) Suppose you work for a large expo organization committee. Please draw up a memorandum that contains the main points according to the given material 3 for the leaders of the organization committee to use in a press briefing on the day of the opening of the expo (10 points). The writing should be concrete and objective, summarizing the information accurately and by category, no more than 200 words.

(d) Please write what inspiration we can we get from the development of China's high-speed rail network, ZTE and China's equipment manufacturing industry based on the given material 4 (20 points). Your statement should center on the given materials and have certain focuses. Make sure that your view is clear, and the statement well founded. No more than 500 words.

(e) In the given material 5, the underlined sentence states that the 'humanization of science and technology' has become an ineradicable feature of the real world, and science and technology will operate within the characteristics of human nature. Please write an essay with a title based on your thoughts on this sentence in combination with social reality (40 points). Your writing should be clear in view and thought provoking. It could draw on, but certainly shouldn't *be bound by, the given materials. Make sure that your writing demonstrates clear thinking and language fluency. The total number of words should be around 1,000-1,200.*

3) Interview

The interview for the admission by exam for cadres is organized and implemented by various employers, but the test contents are designed in a unified way. Since the introduction of a regulated test design, the types, procedures and methods for the interview for all localities and departments are essentially the same. The interview comprises a structured interview and group discussion without leadership presence.

(a) Structured interview

Most of the employers adopt a structured interview as the main form of the interview. The structured interview is conducted according to unified standards and requirements, such as the composition of the test, evaluation elements, assigning scores, time control, adjudication panel, implementation of the procedures and calculation of results. In the course of the question-and-answer interview, the adjudicators observe, judge and evaluate the candidate's qualifications and competence according to their performance and behavior.

The adjudicators are responsible for testing and evaluating the candidates and assigning scores in the structured interview. The panel of adjudicators consists of relevant leaders, experts and cadres in charge of personnel. There are usually at least five people in the panel. Before the interview, the adjudicators need to participate in special training.

The length of time allotted to the interview is generally about 25 minutes. Usually, candidates are required to read relevant materials prepared in advance (the time for reading is not counted in the length of time for the interview). They then need to answer the adjudicators' specific questions concerning different testing and evaluation elements. There are generally about five or six questions.

The chief adjudicator is responsible for asking questions according to the test pamphlet for the structured interview. He is also responsible for reading the guidance, stipulating the number of questions, answer sequence, time allotment and other considerations. He should pay special attention to the appropriateness of the applicant's language and manner. The chief adjudicator asks questions according to the question sequence, while the candidate answers them in the same order. In accordance with the design of the structured interview, the chief adjudicator is responsible for making necessary detailed inquiries. The chief adjudicator should thank the candidate after he finishes answering all the questions. Then, the candidate leaves and the evaluation of his performance begins.

The testing and evaluation elements and the standard for the evaluation are structured in design. Every adjudicator should conduct the observance and assign scores on his own based on consideration of the different elements of the test. After that, the adjudicator should sign his name. Invigilators collect the score sheets from every adjudicator and give them to the scorer for him to calculate the results under the supervision of the supervisors. The adjudicators, scorers and the supervisors put their signatures on the summary sheet, and finally all the records are filed.

The evaluation elements of the structured interview include synthesis, adjustment capacity, initiative (responsibility), plan and organization, communication, verbal expression and behavior. Synthesis mainly measures a candidate's capacity to solve problems by using reasoning methods such as induction and deduction to accurately understand the very nature of matters and the intrinsic relationships between them; adjustment capacity measures a candidate's capacity to promptly and flexibly shift perspective, adjust to changing circumstances, and comprehend by analogy so as to make the right judgment and take action, considering and tackling the problems under stressful circumstances; initiative measures a candidate's capacity to grasp the opportunity to make discoveries or innovate and to do things that don't deteriorate under pressure, which will help improve their job performance or reduce the possibility that problems might occur; plan and organization measures a candidate's capacity to come up with a plan, deploy resources and mediate effectively between parties in conflict concerning their own activities or those of their colleagues or department, based on a set goal; communication measures a candidate's capacity to understand others, clearly express himself and effectively influence others; verbal expression measures a candidate's capacity to talk concisely about their own ideas or viewpoints for different audiences; finally, there are requirements concerning a candidate's behavior and manners.

(b) Group discussion without leadership presence

Some employers also put on a group discussion without leadership present, or combine it with the structured interview. The aim is to conduct a collective test for candidates. They design questions related to the positions and divide candidates into groups according to the positions applied for, with six to eight people for each group. With no leaders present, candidates are allowed to have a free discussion for a certain length of time. Base on their discussion, employers can check each candidate's capacity to coordinate, synthesize, adjust, handle interpersonal relationships and conduct nonverbal communication. It also allows them to investigate their personalities and style of action so as to make an evaluation of the capacities of various candidates.

The group discussion involves many adjudicators and many interviewees. The examination content and evaluation elements of the interview are the same, but group discussion and the structured interview are quite different in terms of the issues discussed and the responses of candidates. Compared with a structured interview, group discussion puts candidates under greater pressure, and draws a response from them that they might replicate in real life. Often, candidates inadvertently demonstrate their various strengths and weaknesses, helping adjudicators make a comparison between them.

(3) Continuous development of the admission by exam for civil servants

1) The legal system for admission by exam continues to develop so as to guarantee the fairness and justice for admission by exam within an institution. In order to regulate the procedures of admission by exam, the Central Organization Department and the Ministry of Personnel jointly issued *Notice on Further Strengthening and Improving the Admission by Exam for Civil Servants of Party Committees and Government Institutions* and other documents in 2003, which aimed to clean up illegal ways of recruitment and make clear stipulations on regulated personnel employment and to increase the objectivity of the examination; in order to regulate recruitment examination work, the Ministry of Personnel and the Ministry of Health jointly issued *General Standard for Physical Checks in the Admission by Exam for Civil Servants (Provisional)* in 2005 and *Manual for Physical Checks in the Admission by Exam for Civil Servants (Provisional)* in 2007, which regulated the items and standards of physical examination, solved problems related to applications of hepatitis B pathogen carrier candidates, and offered a legal basis for the physical examination.

2) Experience is constantly summed up to improve the objectivity of the examination. In practice, all localities and departments constantly

optimize the contents of the civil service examination, increase the ability to evaluate and investigate, intensify efforts to collect, sort out and analyze basic information and data, and improve the standard for evaluating a candidate's competence, with the division of category and hierarchy, in accordance with the requirement for competence and quality for positions defined by category and hierarchy; in essay tests, the method of grading the test online was popularized, which helped reduce errors caused in grading subjective questions; a civil service database of experts at national and provincial level has been established; an interviewer certificates system was implemented, and efforts were made to train the examiners. Since the implementation of the interviewer qualification system in 2002, central state bodies alone have trained up to 10,000 examiners; it is regulated that the number of holders of the civil service examination interviewer qualification certificate issued by civil service departments at provincial level and above or those who have gained a personnel training certificate accounted for no less than 70% of the total number of interview examiners, to ensure that interview work is carried out in a scientific and regulated manner.

3) Grassroots working experience has been given more importance, which has intensified efforts to select talent and encourage students to serve in departments at the grassroots level. Central authorities took the lead in recruiting staff such as college graduate village officials from departments at the grassroots level, selecting through a public selection mechanism from departments at the grassroots level a large number of outstanding young cadres who are capable of doing good mass work, properly dealing with complicated situations and tackling real problems to work in leading bodies of the party and government. This move helped improve the pool size of possible recruits and experience structure of civil servants in central bodies, and ensured that cadres are drawn from the masses and work for the masses. In 2011, the number of civil servants who had more than two years of grassroots work experience accounted for 86% of all those hired by central bodies and their provincial institutions. The system of the railway police targeted the recruitment of civil servants directly from outstanding workers. At the same time, college graduates are recruited to work for the posts below county level. In 2011, it was required that posts in departments at the level below the county were filled mainly by fresh college graduates.[5]

---

[5] *Outlook for 2012: Guidelines for Admission of Civil Servants for Central State Organs*, Sheng Ruowei, People's Daily, October 11, 2011

Special column: The admission by exam for civil servants of the national civil service – the only path to politics

On February 22, 2012, in the grand conference room of the Ministry of Finance on the sixth floor of the north building, 20 young people were sitting – dressed in suits, looking serious, obviously uneasy – all waiting to be interviewed for the 2012 admission by exam for civil servants held by the Ministry of Finance.

Xiao Guo, of humble origin, was the first to take the third-round interview in the afternoon. After a 10-minute preparation for reading the test materials in the preparation area, she walked into the examination room where seven interviewers were sat in a line, in addition to a supervisor, a timekeeper and a score keeper. After the chief interviewer gave a detailed introduction of the interview content, time length and requirements, the interview started.

The interview is divided into two parts, a public aptitude test and professional aptitude test. "The topic is very reasonable," she said. "Whether it is the public capacity test or the professional test, the civil service test must have a test of this quality." Out of the examination room, Xiao Guo said the interview did not surprise her very much. She is confident of getting through.

Over the next three days, the Ministry of Finance would, in accordance with the unified standard process, hold 28 interviews for up to 200 candidates.

"From content to process design, priority is given to justice and fairness," said Nie Shengkui, general director of the exam admission department of the State Administration of Civil Service. "All examiners and candidates must sign a confidentiality agreement. In the same test environment and process, a candidate's true capacity is easily measured."

The strict design of all aspects of the interview illustrates the fair and impartial scientific value orientation of the civil service exam admission system. With reporters there to observe the interview, people can witness the perfect transparency of the whole process. In fact, with unremitting efforts for more than 10 years, this system has always safeguarded talent selection in the PRC, choosing qualified national civil servants.

Liu Xitang, born in rural Hebei and today deputy director of the social assistance department of the Ministry of Civil Affairs, is a beneficiary of this system. In 1995, when he went to Beijing alone to look for a job, it never occurred to him to get a post in a central state body. "At that time, I planned to get a job in a school or a publishing house," says Liu. "Only accidentally did I learn that I could apply to take an exam to join the national civil service."

Without even knowing what he was to be tested on, Liu Xitang just went to the examination room. After two rounds of examinations, he was lucky enough to be admitted to the Ministry of Civil Affairs. Not until later did Liu Xitang realize that it was his background that got him recruited for the rural work. In his journey from the countryside to university, and then to state institutions, Liu Xitang had three deep conclusions: "First, to do rural work better one needs to understand the grassroots and to have a good grasp of the real circumstances of peasants; second, to do rural work better one needs to be devoted to the task, and the fact is that rural work is not that difficult and peasants are particularly easy to approach; third, to do rural work better one needs to have an attitude of cherishing the opportunity to be a civil servant."

"In fact, I was not only a witness of the civil service examination, but also a beneficiary," says Ji Shaoqin, consultant at the science and technology education department under the Ministry of Agriculture. "The exam system for admission to the national civil service has been under development for years. In the past, an interviewer could keep asking questions, but in so doing, he might be biased and act randomly. Today, the interview has strict procedures and regulations, and is impartial to every candidate."

For a fair and scientific evaluation of the exam admission system for civil servants, the Institute of the Chinese Academy of Personnel Sciences set up a special task group. From May 2009 to June 2011, this group conducted a follow-up survey of the development of the exam system for civil servants in central state bodies. The result showed that more than 80% of respondents agreed that the existing work was fair and scientific.

"The existing system of admission by exam for civil servants is improving all the time and the existing process guarantees fairness and justice," says Liu Xitang. "Administrative departments of civil servants are responsible for the written examination, admission by exam agencies participate in the interview, while disciplinary inspection and supervision departments and higher authorities execute supervision. There is a balance of power between them. Meanwhile, the composition of interviewers in every round is decided by drawing lots. Given the large number of interviewers and the random nature of selecting them, it is almost impossible to seek advantage through connections or influence. How can one pull strings when the interviewer himself doesn't even know what test room he will be assigned to?"

"The continuous development of the civil service exam system improves the process of identifying and selecting the best talent across different social strata, which is hard to achieve," says Wu Jiang, president of the Chinese Academy of Personnel Science. He also believes that, given the increasing transparency of the whole process, admission by exam work is becoming more standard and involves supervision from all sectors of society. The system of the admission by exam for civil servants takes root in the heart of the people and is widely accepted by society.[6]

2. Public selection for civil servants in office

Becoming a national civil servant means being a member of the rank of cadres. In order to optimize the talent base of leading cadres and establish the training and selection mechanism of civil servants coming from the grassroots, the organization department of the CPC Central Committee, the Ministry of National Human Resources and Ministry of Social Security jointly issued *Methods for the Public Selection of Civil Servants (Provisional)* in January 2013, activating the selection system of civil servants.

The 'public selection' of civil servants refers to the selection of civil servants from bodies at the grassroots level by their superior bodies at or above the city (prefecture) level. It is the channel that upper-level bodies use to enrich their grassroots work experience and an important approach to select grassroots civil servants for bodies at the upper level. The selection consists of a transfer between bodies without changing a civil servant's rank or promotion. Transfer between bodies without changing a civil servant's rank means selecting civil servants for bodies at the upper level without changing their original position or rank, while promotion means selecting civil servants for bodies at the upper level where a staff member is promoted to a senior staff member and where a senior staff member is promoted to a principal staff member, somewhat like public selection within bodies. But any civil

---

[6] See *More than 80% of Newly Hired Civil Servants Come from Ordinary Families*, Sheng Ruowei, Du Rong, People's Daily, March 2, 2012

servant who wants to participate in public selection should have more than two years grassroots work experience and two years of work experience as a civil servant, and some posts need no less than two years of work experience in his incumbent post.

Each year, the CPC Central Committee, state bodies, all ministries, and party committees and government agencies at above city (prefecture) level should regularly carry out public selection of civil servants according to the following procedures:

(a) announcement;

(b) registration and qualification inspection;

(c) examination;

(d) investigation;

(e) decision and appointment.

In fact, the public selection of civil servants mainly adopts examination to replace the conventional practice of selection and appointment through recommendation. In accordance with the regulations, bodies at the upper level can adopt public selection only in cases when there are no suitable candidates for particular positions that need to be supplemented with those who have grassroots work experience. At the same time, it is impossible to select cadres through recommendation because so many candidates participate in the public selection of civil servants. Examination, therefore, is a natural and inevitable consequence. Yet the result of examination is by no means the only way to select civil servants. To get selected, one needs to withstand the necessary investigation from the organization, including into a candidate's political quality, professional ethics, work capacity and work experience.

The examination of the public selection of civil servants introduces classification and ranking, according to the ranks of position and job categories. Examination is implemented by civil service authorities in a unified and organized way. Endorsed by the civil service authority, the interview can be carried out by departments for their own recruitment through public selection.

The examination is divided into a written examination and interview. Written examination mainly measures a candidate's overall capacity, which includes understanding policy and theory, analyzing and solving practical problems, and writing skills. The number of candidates qualified for interview is decided by a set proportion (generally higher than 5:1) in descending order. The interview mainly measures the basic quality and capacity that the position requires. The content and manner of the interview should be determined according to the characteristics and requirements of each position. If necessary, a test for professional skills can also be adopted. The overall result is determined according to the results of the written examination and interview and the weight of attributes stipulated in the announcement. The result of the written examination, interview and the overall result should be informed to the candidates in time.

(1) Written examination

Compared with the admission by exam for civil servants, the public selection examination places more emphasis on matching the person and the post, and stresses practicality. The test focuses more on the writing skills and capacity to tackle actual problems. The test items are mainly composed of case analysis, essay writing and policy paper writing.

> Example: ***Case analysis (40 points): Answer questions based on the given written material***
>
> *Main idea of the given material: a government conducted political participation through television, covering fields such as education, health care and livelihood issues and it has made some actual impact. On the whole, the social views are positive but there are negative voices as well.*
>
> *1). Please give a brief analysis of and comment on the government's use of live television to implement public supervision over government management. (no more than 400 words)*
>
> *2). What are your suggested measures to improve public supervision over government management though live television? A detailed description of specific and workable measures is needed. (no more than 400 words)*
>
> Example: ***Policy paper writing (60 points)***
>
> *Background materials: 1. the eight rules of the CPC Central Committee; 2. improvement of work style in all localities and departments; 3. remarks on the improvement of work style among society; 4. recent social concern of or discussion about work style.*

Examinees are required to put forward measures and suggestions for party committees and government agencies to improve the long-term mechanism aimed at improving work style and closer ties with the public based on the essential needs of these tasks. Requirements: (1) offer a profound understanding of the problem and put forward measures that meet national and political conditions; (2) emphasis on the discussion about suggestions; (3) make sure that the structure of the thesis is complete, the logical relationship is reasonable, and the expression is accurate, concise and smooth. About 1500 - 1200 words.

Special topic: Essay tests (*shen lun*) and policy paper writing (*ce lun*)

Going back to China's ancient imperial examination system, the essay tests and policy paper writing are means used to evaluate a candidate's capacity to judge and conduct literal expression by writing. But essay writing and political paper writing are quite different from the writing in language tests (TOEFL for example) in that they stress more on the capacity to analyze and solve problems.

Literally, '*shen* (申)' means extension and representation, '*ce* (策)' means policy and strategy, and '*lun* (论)' means discussion and demonstration. Essay tests (*shen*) require candidates to put forward their views on specific issues, and then discuss them in detail, while policy paper writing (*ce*) requires candidates to put forward their own questions concerning specific policies and then demonstrate them.

Essay tests and policy paper writing are often used in the admission by exam for civil servants, competition and public selection. The common characteristics they share is that candidates are required to answer questions after reading given written materials and cases. Both stress the measurement of their professionalism and capacity in actual work. But there are differences and respective focuses. In essay tests, candidates are required to analyze, judge, process and reason about the given materials that reflect existing problems to locate the laws, find ways to solve problems and give a detailed exposition and argumentation of their views. In policy paper writing, the given materials are about the nation's established policies, regulations and solutions to specific problems; candidates are required to discuss the rationality, feasibility and objectivity of the related policies and solutions, find their deficiencies and problems, come up with improved measures and suggestions, and give a full exposition of their own suggestions and illustrate their rationality and feasibility.

(2) Interview

The public selection interview also uses a structured interview. The interview mainly examines civil servants' theoretical policy knowledge, and their capacity to conduct a holistic analysis, to organize and coordinate, to express orally and to deal with emergencies, and other factors such as a candidate's personality, deportment and poise, and special capacities are also covered. The public selection interview is basically the same as the admission by exam for civil servants' interview in terms of composition of procedures, evaluation contents and application of the results, only slightly different from the latter in that the former places more emphasis on the candidate's capacity in actual work because the candidates in question are in-service civil servants who have experience in civil service work.

3. Competition and public selection for leadership posts

Competition for posts and public selection is one of the ways of the selection and appointment of leading cadres in the party and governments. On the basis of the routine cadre selection procedures, competition for posts and public selection has added the process of evaluation and examination. When there are vacancies in leadership positions in some agencies of the party and government, and there are too many qualified candidates so it is hard to unanimously choose candidates from within the agencies, competition for the posts is a good option. Competition for the posts requires that cadres are selected through evaluation and examination based on democratic recommendation, so that the more outstanding cadres stand out.

When a vacancy arises for a leadership position in an agency and there are no suitable candidates, especially those in need of special talent, public selection outside the agency or department can be tried. Public selection uses evaluation and examination as an alternative to democratic recommendation to supply a group of highly talented cadres through large-scale selection. Nevertheless, public selection still lays stress on the nearby talent pool – candidates from other provinces are generally not considered when selecting leading cadres for agencies and departments below county level. When selecting cadres at prefecture level and of bureau rank, selection is generally carried out within the municipality (district).

Competition for posts and public selection is organized and implemented by organization (personnel) departments. Their basic procedures include: (i) announcing the position vacancy, qualifications, basic procedures and methods; (ii) registration and qualification review, anyone who wants to apply for public selection shall get the approval of his work unit; (iii) adopt appropriate means to test and evaluate a candidate's abilities and quality, to compare and sift (democratic recommendation could also be allowed before competition for the posts); (iv) organize the investigation, study and put forward a solution for the final decision; (v) party committees (party groups) discuss the decision; (vi) implement necessary procedures to take the position.

Evaluation and examination in the competition for posts and public selection mainly involve checking a candidate's capacities and qualities, assessing his major achievements and daily work performance and closely centering on the characteristics and requirements of the positions. Methods adopted by such work include written examination, interview, group discussion without leadership presence, evaluation of work experience, work performance and psychological test.

(1) Written examination

The Central Organization Department has specially formulated the *Syllabus of Public Selection and Competition for Leading Cadres of the Party and the Government*. Clear scope has been drawn up for the content of the written examination, which is divided into written examinations on public and professional subjects.

The written examination of public subjects tests the basic professionalism needed for leadership positions, especially the capacity to use basic theories, basic knowledge and basic methods to analyze and solve real problems in leadership work. Evaluation factors of this examination include political theory literacy, public knowledge literacy, policy and regulation attainment, and the capacity to analyze, solve problems and write.

The written examination of professional subjects tests a candidate's professionalism needed for the position, especially his ability to use professional knowledge and theoretical analysis to solve practical problems in leadership work. Evaluation factors of this written examination consist of professional knowledge, understanding of profession-related policies and regulations, professional management skills and other capacities related to position. Specific evaluation factors are determined according to the requirements and analysis of various positions.

Written examination is mainly conducted using paper and pen, but the written examination requiring the use of a computer is also used. The maximum score of the written examination of public subjects is 100 or 150, and the time length is 150 or 180 minutes.

The questions of the written examination are divided into two categories: objective and subjective. Objective questions include judgment questions, choice questions and so on. Subjective questions include essay writing and policy paper writing. The type of questions of this test and that of the admission by exam of cadres are similar, but the content of the former is more on theoretical knowledge and practical capacity.

(2) Interview

The interview is conducted in the form of structured interview, semi-structured interview and group discussion without leadership presence. Compared with the interview for civil service membership, that for leading cadres focuses more on management and leadership. Therefore, evaluation factors have a large scope, including the capacity to conduct comprehensive analysis, to express verbally, to organize and coordinate, to communicate, to make decisions, to innovate, to cope with emergencies, and some special abilities and personality traits specially needed for the posts (such as a candidate's emotional stability, responsibility, self-confidence, achievement motivation and self-cognition). The procedures and types of questions in the structured interview and group discussion without leadership presence and those in the admission by exam for civil servants are basically the same. The semi-structured interview integrates new contents such as continuous questioning and personalized questions.

(3) Experience and performance analysis

The experience and performance analysis originated from background analysis. In the evaluation of competitive selection, local organization departments turned background analysis into experience and performance analysis according to the work situation of cadres of the party and government. Experience and performance analysis can make up for the shortcomings of the written examination, interview and other one-off and terminative evaluation and ensure a fully objective knowledge of the morality and performance of cadres, so as to help enhance credibility and quality in selecting and recruiting candidates.

The experience and performance analysis mainly consists of three dimensions, including experience in learning, education and training, experience in work and work performance. Each dimension is composed of two parts: an objective score assignment and subjective evaluation, of which 60% of the total is normally accounted for by the objective score assignment. The first dimension 'learning and education' experience investigates the extent to which a candidate's experience in learning, education and training is conducted in a complete, systematic and progressive way and that their learning and education background matches the positions. The former is an objective index, while the latter is a subjective evaluation index. The second dimension 'work experience' evaluates to what extent the work experience of the candidates is difficult and that this experience matches the position. The objectivity index of this dimension refers to the score assignment according to the complexity of work experience. Its specific indicators include grassroots work experience, grassroots leadership experience, ranking of the post, title and length of tenure, so as to reflect objectively the richness and complexity of the candidates' work experience. Subjective evaluation refers to the score assignment for a candidate's eligibility according to the correlation degree of the industry and sector. The third dimension 'work performance' evaluates a candidate's work achievements and to what extent they match the position. The objective index of this dimension refers to the score assignment according to a candidate's annual assessment and awards and honors. The scores should take into account the characteristics of the sector and industry where the candidate works, and factors such as the quantity and hierarchy of sectors that issue the awards and honors. Index of work achievement and key performance evaluation refers to the score assignment according to the status of a candidate and the role he plays in actual work. Scores are proportional to the workload and innovation of the candidate. Eligibility analysis refers to the score assignment according to the work performance.

In order to ensure the authenticity and accuracy of personal information, candidates should not only sign a letter of integrity, but also provide physical proof including official seal showing their academic degree, work experience, professional title (occupational qualification), annual assessment, awards and honors, professional achievements and so on. The personnel departments where the candidates work should provide papers and materials verifying their personal experience and work performance and the party committee (group) should be responsible for this verification, ensuring its authenticity and credit.

(Source: http://yn.yunnan.cn/html/2013-07/02/content_2789133.htm)

Experience and performance analysis is used to evaluate a candidate's day-to-day work performance as well as his ability to study in selecting leading cadres. In future, the selection and appointment of leading cadres will place more emphasis on evaluating the usual work and performance of cadres. The effectiveness and feasibility of similar methods are still in the process of exploration and research.

(4) Evaluation of administrative capacity and leadership

The examination and evaluation center of the Central Organization Department has developed a system to effectively evaluate the leadership of leading cadres and for the competitive selection and appointment of leading cadres.

This system refers to a scenario simulation judgment test based on item response theory and a computer adaptive test. Using case scenarios of leading cadres as the evaluation content of this system, candidates are required to conduct grading evaluation on the effectiveness of various solutions in each case on the computer, so as to evaluate the capacities of leading cadres in certain aspects. Test content is closely related to the actual work of leading cadres, mainly evaluating a candidate's capacity to analyze and solve practical problems in leadership work.

The theoretical foundation of the scenario simulation judgment test is not complicated. It is a combination of situational and behavioral interview questions. When candidates deal with the same or similar problems in scenario simulation, their actual behavior in work can be predicted by their behavior in this test. Through the work and questions of scenario simulation, interviewers can pass judgment on the capacities of candidates by comparing their performance in these real or simulated situations with the excellent performance (standard) or average performance (normal) of other people, thus effectively anticipating their work performance in the actual situation.

Example: *Evaluation of administrative capacity and leadership*

One of your subordinates requests a conversation with you, wanting to report problems with some of your other subordinates along with problems in the offices under their leadership. You have been appointed to your current post for just one year, and you have no conflicts with your subordinates. You have established a policy of 'encouraging the free airing of views' for the departments under your leadership, but also hope that cadres can report to their immediate superior before discussing it with others. In view of the sensitivity of the issues he is talking about, he has not talked with his immediate superior (also your subordinate).

Please make an evaluation of the effectiveness of the following practices on a measuring stick ranging from 1 to 7, with 1 meaning very poor and 7 very good:

A. refuse to meet this cadre, unless he talks first with your subordinate;

B. meet the cadre in the presence of your subordinate;

C. meet this cadre first then your subordinate, so as to solicit both their views;

D. meet this cadre first then your subordinate before you investigate the views of the former;

E. collect more information on this cadre before making a decision;

F. refuse to meet this cadre and tell your subordinate that this cadre wants to disrupt the normal process;

G. seek first advice from your superior whom you respect before deciding whether or not to meet this cadre;

H. criticize this cadre to his face on the grounds that he is disrupting the normal process.

Finally, it should be pointed out that competition and public selection is just one of the ways, but surely not the major way, of selecting and appointing leading cadres of the party and government, only adopted from time to time when there is vacancy in leadership positions, and there aren't any suitable candidates arising through democratic recommendation. In addition, good inspection should be made in order to carry out public selection and competition for posts. The inspection shouldn't be neglected on account of, or replaced by test and evaluation. To decide on the most suitable object of inspection one needs to meticulously study and analyze the results of the test and evaluation, and take into account what's going on daily, what the cadre does, and how the candidate matches the position, and in so doing prevent a selection process that only takes scores into account.

Chapter 7

Assessment and Evaluation in the Selection and Appointment of Cadres

In the CPC's cadre management system, the selection and appointment of cadres, along with their education and training, evaluation and assessment, and supervision and management are interrelated important components. Of these four elements, evaluation and assessment is designed to provide a comprehensive evaluation of the character, aptitude and performance of cadres, and is also an important condition and premise for selection and appointment. Therefore, selection and appointment cannot be separated from evaluation and assessment. In the process of selection and appointment, apart from examining how cadres match positions by using methods such as investigation and evaluation, other important elements include annual assessment, examination of performance, special item examination (mainly about assessing a cadre's character) and comprehensive evaluation.

1. Targeted assessment of the morality of cadres

Adhering to the principle of selecting and appointing cadres by evaluating their ability and morality with priority given to the latter is the fundamental requirement and an important guarantee for Marxist political parties to maintain their advanced nature. In the work of selecting and appointing and evaluating and assessing cadres of party organizations and government bodies, the leading role is consistently given to the evaluation of a cadre's morality. In order to implement the principle of selecting and appointing cadres by evaluating their ability and morality, with priority given to the latter, and make an overall, objective and accurate assessment of cadres and establish the correct guidance for selection and appointment, the Organization Department of the Central Committee of the CPC promulgated *Notes on the Strengthening of Evaluation of the Morality of Our*

Cadres in 2011, emphasizing the strengthened assessment of cadres, making a scientific summary of the historical experience in the work of selection and appointment of party cadres, and constituting the requirement of adhering to and implementing the principle of selecting and appointing cadres by evaluating their ability and morality, with priority given to the latter, under the new historical conditions. It must proceed from the vantage point of maintaining the party's advanced nature and purity, from the practical needs of building a contingent of high quality cadres, highlighting the leading role of morality in the standard for cadres, and establishing the correct orientation that advocates making use of morality to cultivate oneself, to convince the public, to guide and develop his ability, and having both ability and morality.

(1) The basic connotation of a cadre's morality

Morality is the basic criterion and standard for a person's everyday life and behavior. The cadre's 'morality' is a synthesis that is multi-level and multi-lateral, with specific connotations. It is rich in content and attributes, needing to be analyzed and understood from different angles and different sides.

At the 2008 national organization work conference, comrade Xi Jinping pointed out that the moral standard of cadres should include the standard of political quality, professional ethics, family virtues and social ethics. In 2009, the fourth plenary session of the 17th CPC Central Committee passed *Decision of the Central Committee of the CPC on Strengthening and Improving the Construction of the Party in the New Situation*, which made it clear that the criterion for evaluating a cadre's morality should be improved in respect of political quality and morality, with stress on whether cadres are loyal to the party, to the country and to the people, on whether they establish a correct world outlook, view of power and concept of career, on whether they have the determination to perform real work, the courage to shoulder responsibility and the determination to forge ahead, and on whether they have moral and healthy interests, and on whether they are clean and honest. 'Decision' centers closely around the party's fundamental purpose and central task, putting forward specific requirements of cadres' morality in the new period from aspects such as ideals and beliefs, political quality, work style and moral character, and further clarifying the key content and evaluation criteria for the inspection of cadres' morality.

In 2011, the Organization Department of the Central Committee promulgated and implemented *Notes on Strengthening the Assessment of Cadres' Morality*, setting out explicitly the requirements for strengthening the assessment of political quality and moral character of leading cadres. The *Notes* pointed out that the assessment of a cadre's morality should embody the professional characteristics and responsibility of national public officials, being in step with the Central Committee of the CPC, moving ahead of the ordinary people and being a good example to the requirements for keeping political, advanced and exemplary in nature, and strengthen the assessment of political quality and moral character with a stress on party loyalty, serving the people and self-discipline. The assessment of the political quality of cadres mainly looks at their performance in aspects such as political orientation, political stance, political attitude, political discipline, party principle, focuses on understanding the extent to which cadres should hold firmly their ideals and faith, adhere to the road, theoretical systems and regulations of socialism with Chinese characteristics, remain loyal to the party, country and the people, implement a scientific outlook on development, the party's line, principles and policies, establish a correct world outlook, view of power, career outlook, practice the party's purpose, adhere to the principles of governing for the people, maintain close ties with the public, stick to general principles, take responsibility and implement democratic centralism. The assessment of the moral character of cadres mainly covers their social morality, professional ethics, personal morality and family virtues, and focuses on understanding the extent to which cadres practice the socialist core value system, comply with social public morality, resist uncivilized behavior, are devoted to their work, do a real job, forge ahead, and stay fair and decent, honest and trustworthy and well-behaved, and are healthy in habits, and in compliance with the code of conduct of clean governance, exercising power justly, staying clean, honest, upright and unselfish, and strictly keeping their spouses, children and other relatives well disciplined.

(2) Evaluation of a cadre's morality

In accordance with the essence of a series of related speeches by the leadership of the Central Committee and the requirements proposed in *Opinions on Strengthening the Assessment of a Cadre's Morality*, the cadres' moral assessment mainly consist of two elements (or dimensions): political quality and moral character. They are the first-grade indicators of the evaluation system. On this basis, it is also necessary to subdivide these first-grade indicators into a number of items as second-grade indicators for operative evaluation. Party organizations across the country have carried out many trials and experiments across the country. These two elements of the evaluation contain the following two second-grade indicators. See table 7-1.

Table 7-1 Contents and structure of the evaluation of the morality of leading cadres of the party and government

Political quality	Moral character
Ideals and beliefs	Professional ethics
Holistic view	Personal morality
Tenet and objectives	Social morals
Work style	Family virtues

In accordance with the requirements proposed in *Opinions on Strengthening the Assessment of a Cadre's Morality*, some assessment focuses should be put forward about a cadre's morality in terms of grades and classification according to the ranking and positions of cadres, on the basis of a comprehensive evaluation. It is committed to determine and establish items of assessment that are focused on and emphasize the actual situation of cadres in various regions, sectors and industry. The basic points of the *Opinions* about the assessment of cadres are: (1) taking a comprehensive evaluation as the premise; (2) highlighting the assessment of the political quality of senior and intermediate cadres, especially party chiefs; (3) highlighting the assessment of sense of purpose, the concept of the public, fairness and justice in handling affairs, work style and so on of leading cadres at the grassroots level.

The evaluation of a cadre's morality is still in the process of development and exploration. In the work of evaluating cadres in all departments, it is the reviewers who usually pass judgment on and evaluate the behavioral characteristics of those under evaluation that reflect the second-grade indicators. These behavioral characteristics should be highly representative and objective. Table 7-2 contains a list of assessment essentials of second-grade indicators, which are behavior characteristics that consist of the specific topics for morality assessment.

Table 7-2 Assessment essentials for a cadre's morality

First-grade indicator	Second-grade indicator	Assessment essentials (behavioral characteristics)
Political quality	Ideals and beliefs	Take firm political stand, stay loyal to the party, the state and the people; believe in the theory of socialism, the socialist road, and the socialist system with Chinese characteristics; remain sober and adopt a clear-cut attitude in front of major issues of right and wrong
	Holistic view	Work around the center, serving the overall interests; subject to the decision and discipline of the organization; unite and work together to maintain the cohesion of the organization and the leadership team
	Tenet and objectives	Always put the people in first place while serving the people; concern and contact with the public, and show feelings for them; safeguard the vital interests, legitimate rights and interests of the public
	Work style	Adhere to democratic centralism; often go to the grassroots and the front-line, and maintain close ties with the public; be good at learning, and constantly improve theoretical quality
Moral character	Professional ethics	Be conscientious and meticulous in work, adhere to general principles and take the initiative in undertaking responsibilities; work whole-heartedly, be brave in taking on heavy responsibilities and do hard and practical work; handle matters impartially, do not be swayed by personal considerations and seek no personal gain
	Personal morals	Be honest and trustworthy, decent and upright; be modest and tolerant and respect others; live frugally and cultivate healthy habits
	Social morals	Take the lead in following public order, and do not engage in privilege; assume social responsibility, and actively participate in public welfare activities; resist all kinds of uncivilized behavior
	Family virtues	Be loyal to one's spouse and family; fulfill the obligations of supporting parents and children; be a good neighbor

(3) Methods for evaluating a cadre's morality

The methods for evaluating a cadre's morality seek to adopt alternative approaches and methods for a comprehensive evaluation based on the basic requirements of the authority of the management of cadres and the assessment and evaluation. The main methods include the evaluation of specific-item morality, and of the morality in democratic evaluation and public opinion polls. The scope of the evaluation starts from within the bodies and spreads outside, involving a cadre's superiors, colleagues, subordinates, the masses who are served by cadres, residential communities, etc., constituting a 360° evaluation model. But in actual work, most units and departments or institutions adopt a 360° evaluation within the institution, rarely involving the masses and community residents for example. In order to evaluate the morality of cadres, a small number of regions explore public opinion surveys gauge the social ethics and family virtues of leading cadres in the streets and communities. For example, some local party committee organization departments printed a *Public Opinion Questionnaire for 'Four Virtues' of Leading Cadres*, in which cadres and local people are required to fill in blank items. In the end, there will be an assessment and evaluation summary table of 'four virtues' for each object of study, providing evidence for a comprehensive analysis of the 'four virtues' of leading cadres. In many regions, they conduct visits to their home, neighborhood and community for those candidates in line for promotion, so as to inspect their performance in areas such as life interests, interpersonal relationships, family and neighborhood relations.

(4) Reverse evaluation

'Reverse evaluation' is one of the most representative and outstanding innovative practices in the evaluation of cadres in all parts of the country. It uses the reverse design or negative evaluation indicators (evaluation essentials) to survey those who are familiar with the objects of study to investigate whether they know something negative about them, in order to provide a comprehensive, accurate and true grasp of a cadre's moral conduct. Its basic assumption and principle is: to grasp the moral conduct of a cadre, one needs to look at both positive and negative reports. To a certain extent, the negative evaluation is more realistic and objective in reflecting the complete picture of a cadre's morality.

Drawing on the reverse questions in psychological evaluation, this method of evaluation is similar to the use of a symptom table in the evaluation of mental health. It makes inference and assesses specific psychological traits of the object of study by judging and evaluating his problematic behaviors or symptoms in terms of specific factors. The evaluation of morality mainly refers to the inference and assessment of the moral character of cadres. In the psychological measurement and evaluation of talent, reverse evaluation is often adopted. One way is to tackle positive and negative questions alternately; another way is to present only negative questions, for example, in order to judge any possible psychological abnormalities of the object of study.

Reverse evaluation items or reverse evaluation essentials are valuable for the improvement of the operability (observable and evaluable) of the evaluation of a cadre's morality. They draw mainly on the outstanding issues closely related to moral character existing in cadres, mainly involving political quality and moral character. Table 7-3 lists the major items of reverse evaluation carried out in various regions.

Table 7-3 Reverse evaluation indicators of the morality of leading cadres (evaluation essentials)

Evaluation essentials	Reverse evaluation essentials
Political quality	Spread speeches or heresies that violate party guidelines and policies
	Be indifferent and ambiguous in the face of major issues of right and wrong
	Be perfunctory, shift blame and shy away from responsibility in the face of danger and crisis
	Put departmentalism and local interests above overall interests
	Fail to adhere to democratic centralism, exercise tyrannical governance, and make conflicts harmful to unity
	Disregard the rights and interests of the masses and grassroots
	Stay aloof from the masses and the grassroots
	Prefer formalism, put on a hollow display, and harass people and waste money
	Strive hard for an official position through dishonest means, or canvass votes and take election bribes
	Use power to seek illegitimate interests for themselves or their relatives

Evaluation essentials	Reverse evaluation essentials
Moral character	Damage the interests of the public and seek gains at their expense
	Fail to comply with public order in public places
	Fail to assume or shirk the required social responsibility
	Have affairs or improper relationships outside marriage
	Love pleasure and comfort, enjoy extravagance and waste, and lead a pompous and lavish life
	Fail to fulfill the obligation of supporting one's parents or raising children
	Be slack in family management, and pamper and indulge relatives
	Fail to have a good relationship with neighbors
	Patronize vulgar places, gamble or become involved in prostitution and other illegal activities
	Form unhealthy habits and get addicted to bad habits

(5) Feedback and application of evaluation results

Generally, the results of the evaluation of a cadre's morality are classified according to four levels: excellent, good, fair and poor, or excellent, good, qualified and unqualified; or five levels: satisfactory, quite satisfactory, basically satisfactory, unsatisfactory and uncertain. Some even use a 100-mark scoring system to replace the above for better comparison and feedback.

Result feedback has always been an important link in the evaluation of cadres, especially when it concerns morality. In some regions, they explored and evaluated the morality of cadres. In some other regions, they explored and implemented a 'one-form model' for feedback on the results of the annual assessment of cadres, making an effective attempt to properly utilize the assessment results. The 'one-form model' requires that feedback on the evaluation results is put into one sheet of 'feedback form for the results of the annual assessment of cadres', sent to cadres under the assessment of the Organization Department.

It concentrates on three types of information: 1. descriptive information, which includes the comprehensive score, score for sub-items and number of votes in the reverse evaluation. The 'comprehensive score' generally uses the 100-mark system, the quantitative results about the democratic evaluation and performance assessment; the score for the sub-items is the result of evaluating the contents of various dimensions or elements, the number of votes in reverse evaluation refers to the original data of the reverse evaluation of the objects by the public and other cadres, which contains the results of reverse evaluation on morality; 2. comparative information that includes descriptive statistic results of the assessment of the contingent (highest score, average score, lowest score), ranking of the assessment for each in the contingent and graphs for the evaluation in terms of their morality, competence, diligence, performance and morality; 3. information for judgment and guidance which refers to the ranking of the annual assessment ranging from excellent, competent, basically competent to incompetent, and giving guidance to those cadres that fare poorly in the assessment, in terms of major advantages, achievements, problems and directions for improvement.

Some places set up a 'critical point' for the evaluation of morality, and explored and established the file system for moral character. Some local party committees explored how to define the 'critical point' for the standard of morality, and implemented the quantitative deduction system for morality, and established the file system for moral character. Some local party committees and organizations proposed that those cadres under inspection who score lower than 80 points in the assessment should be subject to a rearranged deliberation before getting promoted and appointed, and the Organization Department should remind them that their work needs to improve; those who score lower than 70 points in the assessment shouldn't be included in the inspection for promotion and appointment, and if they have already been included, the process should be suspended immediately; those who score lower than 60 points in the assessment should be subject to persuasion and admonishment about morality, and not be promoted in the short term; those cadres who score lower than 60 points in the assessment for two consecutive years should be replaced swiftly according to the procedures of the organization. The classification of different measures for education, training, supervision and management according to the evaluation results of a cadre's morality will ensure the effective application of the results of the evaluation of morality.

2 Annual examination of cadres

The annual examination of cadres is a comprehensive evaluation of cadres in terms of their performance in morality, abilities and work during the year. The annual assessment is not only an important way to assess cadres, but also an important part of the inspection of cadres, providing a crucial reference for the selection and appointment of cadres.

The annual assessment of cadres is divided into two categories according to the objects of assessment: the annual assessment of leading cadres in the party and government, and the annual assessment of other civil servants. The requirements of the annual assessment vary with the positional responsibilities. The annual assessment of leading cadres places emphasis on work performance.

(1) Annual assessment of leading cadres

On July 16, 2009, the Organization Department of the CPC Central Committee issued *Methods for the Annual Assessment of Leading Bodies and Leading Cadres in the Party and Governments (Provisional)*. Consisting of 15 items, the document chooses as its objects of evaluation the collective leadership and its members in departments and internal institutions of the party committee and government agencies such as party committees of the CPC at all levels, the Standing Committees of the People's Congress, government agencies, the CPPCC, the Party Disciplinary Committees of the CPC, the people's court and people's procuratorates.

The main contents of the annual assessment consist of morality, abilities and work performance. The annual assessment of the collective leadership (leading bodies) mainly refers to the assessment of the actual situation of how its functional role has been fulfilled, with the contents of assessment including the actual results in aspects such as ideological and political construction, leadership, work performance, fulfillment of key tasks and the anti-corruption campaign. The personal annual assessment of leading cadres in the party and government mainly refers to the assessment of how job duties have been performed during the year, with its contents including real performance in aspects such as morality, abilities, diligence and performance.

The main means of the annual assessment consists of a debriefing report on one's work and evaluation. The assessment procedures generally include the following:

* * It requires that materials such as personal debriefing reports of leading cadres and fulfillment of annual objectives should be issued in advance, for reviewers to form a comprehensive understanding of and balanced information about the actual work of the subjects.

* It involves a meeting for democratic evaluation. This meeting is chaired by the main person in charge of the party committee, attended by the heads of personnel departments of the party committee and organization at the upper level, leading cadres of certain ranks and ordinary staff representatives within the institution, and all the staff in relatively small institutions if possible. In the meeting for democratic evaluation, senior leaders in the party and governments or departments deliver leadership work summary and personal debriefing reports while other members of the collective leadership deliver personal debriefing reports or provide their written debriefing reports. Those who participate in the evaluation should fill out the evaluation form that is designed according to the basic requirements of the assessment of cadres. The evaluation of cadres in terms of moral character, ability, behavior and performance are graded as excellent, competent, basically competent and incompetent, or good, relatively good, barely good and poor. Personnel departments at the upper level or within the institution are responsible for collecting the evaluation form, compiling statistics, providing feedback and putting the form into the personal files of cadres.

Table 7-4 Evaluation form for the annual assessment of cadres

Dimensions of evaluation	Evaluation indicators	Rankings of evaluation
Morality	Political morality	[A][B][C][D]
	Work style	[A][B][C][D]
	Moral character	[A][B][C][D]
Abilities	Work approaches	[A][B][C][D]
	Team construction	[A][B][C][D]
	Professional competence	[A][B][C][D]
Diligence	Mindset	[A][B][C][D]
	Work engagement	[A][B][C][D]
Performance	Fulfillment of annual routine tasks	[A][B][C][D]
	Fulfillment of annual key tasks	[A][B][C][D]
Morality	Personal morality	[A][B][C][D]
	Fulfillment in building a clean and honest government	[A][B][C][D]
Comprehensive evaluation		[A][B][C][D]

Democratic evaluation in the annual assessment is a way of assessing cadres with striking Chinese characteristics. Different from the practice of evaluating cadres by their superiors widely used elsewhere in the world, democratic evaluation refers to a 360° evaluation of cadres in terms of the degree of satisfaction. It not only includes the evaluation of the performance of cadres (based on their debriefing reports), but also the evaluation of their attitudes, abilities and behavior. It involves various aspects, thus forming a comprehensive evaluation of all aspects and many perspectives.

* The results of the assessment are not entirely decided by the results of the democratic evaluation. The annual assessment seeks to analyze the actual work of the evaluation of various subjects and rankings in accordance with qualitative and quantitative methods and according to the results of classification and division and comprehensive statistics in the annual assessment of leading bodies and leading cadres. It conducts a comprehensive analysis of leading bodies and leading cadres combined with the annual summary, individual discussion and usual assessment to form final opinions of the annual assessment ranked as: excellent, competent, basically competent and incompetent.

* The *Methods for the Annual Assessment of Leading Bodies and Leading Cadres in the Party and Government (Provisional)* clearly stipulates that the opinions of the annual assessment shall be an important basis for strengthening leading bodies and the selection and appointment, training and education, management and supervision, incentives and restraints of leading cadres. In specific operation, leading cadres graded as excellent in the annual assessment are given public recognition. Should leading cadres fail to win two thirds of the vote for the recognition of excellence and competence in the annual assessment and be found incompetent by the organizational assessment, they must be subject to admonishment or transfer to another department. Should leading cadres fail to win one third of the votes for the recognition of competence in the annual assessment and be found incompetent by the organizational assessment, they must be subject to dismissal, resignation or demotion, depending on the specific circumstances.

(2) Annual assessment of regular civil servants

The annual assessment of common leading cadres and common civil servants in the internal institutions of party committees and government agencies is carried out in accordance with the *Regulations on the Assessment of Civil Servants (Provisional)*. This document proposes regulations on the use of the contents, standards, procedures, application of the results, and so on for the annual assessment of common civil servants. It was jointly issued in 2007 by the Central Organization Department of the CPC Central Committee and the Ministry of Human Resources and Social Security.

The annual assessment of civil servants is also carried out at the end of each year or the beginning of the following year. But the contents and methods of assessment are quite different from those of the assessment of leading cadres. Generally, common civil servants are exempted from an annual evaluation. Only those under assessment need to provide a summary in accordance with their positions, responsibilities and relevant requirements, and deliver debriefing reports on their work to a limited extent; based on listening to the opinions of the people and civil servants, supervisors-in-charge at the upper level write a comment, suggest an assessment ranking and proffer requirements for improvement according to the usual assessment and personal summary; finally, persons-in-charge within the agency or an authorized committee of assessment decide the assessment ranking; a written notice of the results of the assessment must be sent to civil servants under assessment for confirmation. If necessary, civil servants assuming leadership in the internal institutions of the bodies can participate in the democratic evaluation to a certain degree. Thus, greater requirements are needed for the assessment of leading cadres than for common civil servants or common cadres. *The Regulations on the Assessment of Civil Servants (Provisional)* stipulate that the results of the annual assessment are divided into four rankings: excellent, competent, basically competent and incompetent. Of the four rankings, an 'excellent' ranking must involve: good ideological and political quality, high professionalism, strong ability, a strong sense of responsibility, diligence, good work style, outstanding work performance and striking honesty and uprightness. A ranking of 'competence' must involve: relatively high political quality, familiarization of work, relatively strong ability, a relatively strong sense of responsibility, high motivation of work, relatively good work style, ability to do regular work, and honesty and self-discipline. Civil servants will be ranked as 'basically competent' under the following circumstances: average ideological and political quality, relatively weak ability to fulfill responsibilities; an average sense of responsibility or an obviously defective work style; those who can basically finish their work but fare poorly in the amount of work and quality and efficiency, or make large errors at work; those who are basically honest and self-disciplined but have problems in some aspects. Civil servants will be ranked as 'incompetent' under the following circumstances: those who have poor ideological and political quality; those whose professional quality and ability are unable to adapt to the requirements of the position; those who have a weak sense of responsibility and bad work style; those who are unable to fulfill the tasks, or commit serious mistakes at work, or cause significant losses or adverse social impact for a neglect of duty; those who have quite serious corruption problems.

The results of the annual assessment of civil servants serve as a reference for the adjustment of the positions, ranks, wages, rewards, training and dismissal of civil servants.

3. Comprehensive evaluation and assessment

As an assessment of cadres during the term of service, comprehensive evaluation refers to a comprehensive evaluation of the performance of duties of cadres in a term of service. It is mainly used for the selection, appointment and deployment of cadres. Specifically, it is used for the inspection of cadres (during the term of service) in leadership transition, and the inspection of promotion and appointment of individual leading cadres. The results of the comprehensive evaluation serve as the main basis for the inspection of cadres before their appointment.

'Comprehensive' refers to the comprehensive analysis of aspects such as usual assessment, annual assessment, inspection of cadres (in the term of service) in leadership transition through the integrated use of methods such as democratic evaluation, public opinion polls, individual conversation, performance analysis and comprehensive evaluation, so as to make a more comprehensive, objective and precise evaluation of leading bodies and leading cadres. Therefore, unlike the single assessment, comprehensive evaluation is the result of combined action of a variety of assessment methods.

In 2009, the Organization Department of the Central Committee promulgated the *Methods for the Comprehensive Evaluation of Leading Bodies and Leading Cadres of the Local Party and Government (Provisional)* and *Methods for the Comprehensive Evaluation of Leading Bodies and Leading Cadres in the Party and Government Departments (Provisional)* for the management of comprehensive evaluation. At present, the assessment of cadres during their terms of office in the party and governments in China is implemented in accordance with the above two documents.

(1) Major features of comprehensive evaluation

Compared with the single assessment, comprehensive evaluation has the following main features:

First, it is a comprehensive inspection. Comprehensive evaluation refers to a comprehensive inspection of leadership abilities of leading bodies and the moral quality and ability of leading cadres. It includes: carrying out quantitative evaluation of various indicators of economic and social development; conducting qualitative evaluation of the extent to which the work of leading bodies and leading cadres is acknowledged and recognized through on-the-spot investigations, extensive inspections and solicited opinions from the informed; and forming opinions of the comprehensive evaluation of both qualitative evaluation and quantitative analysis based on comprehensive judgments.

Second, it is the expansion of democracy. Comprehensive evaluation embodies more democracy and transparency in the assessment of cadres. It ensures participation and representation of various interests by combining evaluation by the relevant functional departments, by the departments where the subjects work, by the grassroots and society. At the same time, emphasizing on extending the right to know, it further publicizes the contents, procedures and methods of assessment; adopts means of democracy and publicity to determine target values and weights of the assessment items; and strengthens the participation and supervision of cadres inside the party and the public outside the party, so as to enhance transparency in the work of assessment.

Third, it involves a diverse source of information. The information and materials of comprehensive evaluation are accredited to multiple aspects, multi-levels, multi-channels and multi-angles. With its overall coordination in charge of the organization and personnel department, it involves many departments, covering statistics, polls, audit and the party and government. In some regions, they have founded the assessment committee led by the organization and personnel departments, responsible for the comprehensive evaluation of leading local cadres. In most regions, they resort to common analysis and research by convening a joint meeting, so as to make an evaluation of work performance of leading bodies and leading cadres of the party and government at lower levels.

Fourth, it is a strengthened application of the results of assessment. Comprehensive evaluation refers to a comprehensive analysis of the situation in aspects such as daily assessment, annual assessment, inspection of cadres (in the term of service) in leadership transition and the inspection of the appointment of individual leading cadres, and the comprehensive evaluation of leading bodies and leading cadres. Therefore, the organization and personnel departments put particular emphasis on the application of the results of assessment in the whole process of the management of cadres. It makes the results of the comprehensive evaluation the basis for selection and appointment, training and education, management and supervision, incentive and restraint of leading bodies and cadres; gives full play to the positive role of assessment; intensifies its efforts to form a correct guidance for recruitment and appointment that focuses on moral character, scientific development, hard work, grassroots experience, innovation and recognition of the general public. Generally, for those who conscientiously adhere to scientific development, exercise good leadership over scientific development, hold steadfast to the principles, dare to tackle and excel at tough matters, perform well at work, and win the recognition of the general public, they are rewarded with awards and promotion; for those who fail to handle affairs in accordance with the outlook on scientific development, seek quick success and instant benefits, engage in formalism and superficial projects, shirk responsibility, disregard principle, avoid offending people, or cause problems when meeting obligatory targets, they are often given critical education, admonishment and are urged to carry out rectification; for those who are found incompetent in their work and fail to win the trust of the general public, a timely adjustment of their positions will be made within the organization in line with the administrative authority of cadres; for those who cause serious consequences because of a dereliction of duty, their acts will be dealt with in strict accordance with laws and disciplinary procedures.

The feedback of the results of comprehensive evaluation will be sent to leading bodies and leading cadres in a timely and objective way. Should the leading bodies and leading cadres disagree with the results of the evaluation of his assessment, they could make a complaint to the organization departments of party committees at upper levels. According to the regulations, these organization departments should follow up in time to investigate and come up with a clear response.

(2) Major means of comprehensive evaluation

Comprehensive evaluation includes democratic evaluation, opinion polls, individual discussions and performance analysis.

1) Democratic evaluation

Democratic evaluation is an evaluation of the behavior within the institutions, mainly referring to soliciting the evaluation of leading bodies about their work and leading cadres about their actual performance from their superiors, colleagues and subordinates. In the system of the evaluation of cadres, democratic evaluation can best embody the spirit of democracy and the justice of procedures.

Democratic evaluation in the assessment is generally carried out at the end of the term of service of leading bodies and leading cadres. For those cadres who are going to be promoted while in the term of service, democratic evaluation will also be needed and carried out.

For leading bodies, democratic evaluation needs to be conducted on the basis of the summary of their work. Its contents and key points are generally set up in accordance with five categories: ideological and political construction, leadership, work performance, anti-corruption and accomplishment of key tasks. The specific contents of the accomplishment of key tasks can be proposed by organization departments of party committees at a higher level, depending on the specific circumstances of the localities and departments. For the leading bodies of party committees, the focuses of the evaluation are on global perspective, coordination of various parties, scientific decision-making, party building, etc.; and for the leading bodies of the government, the focuses of the evaluation are on global perspective, focusing capacity, promotion and implementation, construction of administrative effectiveness and capacity, etc.

For leading cadres of the party and government, democratic evaluation is carried out based on debriefing reports of their work and morality. Generally, the contents and key points of the evaluation are set up according to the classification of morality, competence, diligence and performance. For the evaluation of leading bodies in party committees, democratic evaluation focuses on aspects such as macro policy, coordination of various parties, team building and basic work. For the evaluation of leading bodies in government, democratic evaluation focuses on evaluation in aspects such as innovation consciousness, division of labor and cooperation, implementation and development, and management of departments. For evaluation of leading cadres in subordinate departments of the party and government, there should be evaluation items with characteristics specific to the departments and positions in accordance with the actual situation of various departments.

Democratic evaluation should not only cover evaluation items, but also make an overall evaluation. The evaluation items and overall evaluation of leading bodies are divided into four rankings: good, relatively good, average and poor. The evaluation items of leading cadres are divided into following rankings: good, relatively good, average and poor. The evaluation of the overall evaluation is divided into these rankings: excellent, competent, basically competent and incompetent.

2) Public opinion survey

The public opinion survey solicits opinions of the general public about the performance of leading bodies and leading cadres of local party committees and the government through evaluation from relevant departments in society. Generally, it takes the form of a questionnaire or makes use of individual interviews and seminars according to the actual situation. The public opinion survey is also an important way to reflect the democracy of the assessment.

The public opinion survey about the leading bodies of local party committees and government includes the improvement of people's livelihood, social harmony, work state and efficiency related to party conduct and government style of the leading cadres in internal institutions of party committees and governments that the general public can directly sense. The public opinion survey about leading cadres of local party committees and governments and the internal institutions of party committees and governments includes the execution of duties, work style and public image. The contents of the public opinion survey can be designed and adjusted based on the specific circumstances in different localities, regions, departments and levels, as well as the outstanding issues raised by the general public.

Different from the democratic evaluation that is carried out in departments or within internal institutions, the public opinion survey entrusts third-party agencies with the task of designing and administering the questionnaire. The subjects of the survey generally cover representatives of congress of the CPC, deputies to the NPC, members of the CPPCC, and the masses that are highly related to and know a lot about the objects of assessment. The number of participants is determined through random sampling according to the actual situation.

3) Individual discussions

Individual discussions are often used in the inspection before an appointment. As an important part of the assessment of cadres, the individual discussions can be used for a more in-depth understanding of leadership team building and a leading cadre's morality, abilities and actual performance, so as to cover a lack of in-depth information in the democratic evaluation and public opinion survey.

Similar to the previous democratic evaluation in contents and essential points, individual discussions have more in-depth contents, and also collect some relevant information besides the evaluation essentials. Generally, it needs a prepared outline and specific key points based on the contents and essential points of the evaluation.

Individual discussions are carried out within the institutions. Their subjects include relevant leaders of the higher authorities and relevant departments (units), principal leading cadres of internal institutions and subordinate units, and other people who need to participate. The discussions will be recorded, and used for the evaluation of the comprehensive evaluation of cadres.

4) Analysis of achievements

Analysis of achievements refers to a comprehensive evaluation of leading cadres based on qualitative and quantitative analysis within and outside institutions.

The contents of the analysis of the achievements of leading bodies and leading cadres of local party committees and governments include: (1) statistics and evaluation indicators covering aspects such as the level of economic development, comprehensive benefits of economic development, urban and rural incomes, regional economic development discrepancy, costs of development, basic education, urban employment, medical and health work, cultural life in urban and rural areas, social security, energy conservation, emission reductions, environmental protection, ecological construction, the protection of cultivated land and other resources, population and family planning, investment in science and technology, and innovation; (2) the results of public opinion polls and the satisfaction of the general public towards the actual local economic and social development; (3) the results of the audit investigation and investigation conclusion and the opinions of evaluation in terms of the audit of economic responsibility, relevant audit and audit of specific items conducted by the audit departments of higher authorities.

The analysis of the achievements of leading bodies and leading cadres of party committees and government and internal government departments at all levels refers to the analysis of performance of duties and the completion of tasks mainly through evaluation from their superiors, relevant functional departments, their own departments, the general public and their own self-evaluation. (1) Evaluation from superiors refers to understanding aspects such as the implementation of decision deployment made by superiors, completion of important tasks, formulation of policies and measures and promotion of reform and innovation by leading bodies and leading cadres, mainly based on the opinions of leaders in charge, and the results of assessment conducted by party committees, governments and competent departments of higher authority; (2) evaluation by relevant functional departments (departments of statistics, audit, environmental protection, inspection, supervision and so on) refers to the understanding of the situation in aspects such as sense of the overall situation, work efficiency, service and management, and government morality of leading bodies and leading cadres, based mainly on materials concerning important statistics of economic and social development, professional morals, government style, inspection of administrative law enforcement, audit of economic responsibility, audit of special items, performance evaluation, assessment of resources and environmental protection, assessment of energy-saving and emission-reduction measures, assessment of the party building work responsibility system, assessment of construction of party conduct and government morality, patrol of inspection teams, which are all regularly provided by functional departments; (3) internal evaluation refers to the understanding of the basic situation of the work performance of leading bodies and leading cadres, based mainly on the results of democratic evaluation; (4) evaluation by the general public refers to the understanding of the degree of satisfaction of service objects and relevant parties of society towards leading bodies and leading cadres, based on the results of public opinion investigation; (5) self-evaluation refers to the understanding of areas such as efficiency in the performance of duties and existing problems, based mainly on the regular (or as the assessment requires) work summary by leading bodies and leading cadres in accordance with the functions of their departments (position descriptions) and work targets.

(3) Overall analysis of comprehensive evaluation

Based on information obtained from multi-channels, multi-levels and through multi-methods, the organization and personnel departments need to collect all kinds of results of qualitative evaluation and quantitative statistics, and complement and confirm each other. Generally, the comprehensive analysis needs to proceed from the following sources of information:

Type analysis This refers to an organized and systematized classification of various materials according to the effects caused by the source materials, occurrence time, contents, object of study, etc.

Data analysis This refers to evaluating the effectiveness of the work and public recognition of the object of assessment by analyzing data formed in links such as the democratic recommendation, democratic evaluation, public opinion polls and analysis of the achievements.

Comparative analysis This refers to the evaluation of the main advantages, disadvantages and expertise of the objects of assessment by making a comparative analysis of similarities and dissimilarities reflected in all processes of assessment, and of the performance of the objects of assessment and other members within leading bodies.

Environmental analysis This refers to the degree of subjective efforts of the objects of assessment by analyzing objective environmental factors of their work performance, and, in particular, work foundation and working conditions.

Historical analysis This refers to the evaluation of the consistent performance and basic quality of the objects of assessment by a combined analysis of the historical situation and current situation.

In some localities and departments, they also quantify the contents and assessment indicators, set the appropriate weight scores and carry out a comprehensive analysis by adopting a quantitative scoring system. Comprehensive evaluation not only contains the results of qualitative evaluation but also takes into account the data of quantitative assessment, current work performance, historic conditions, environmental basis and delayed impact. Thus, it ensures the formation of the objective and comprehensive results of the evaluation of assessment of leading bodies and leading cadres.

4 Usual assessment of cadres

The assessment of civil servants is divided into regular and daily assessment. The regular assessment includes an annual assessment and comprehensive evaluation at the end of the term of office. In addition to this regular assessment, the daily assessment of cadres can also provide a good objective basis and important reference for the selection and appointment of cadres. In fact, regular assessment takes usual assessment as its basis.

Daily assessment generally refers to the review and evaluation by leaders in charge of departments at a higher level, in terms of work summary of the objects under assessment, inspection of their specific work and attendance, with stress on their completion of daily tasks, goals at different stages and attendance. In recent years, in order to improve scientific quality in the selection and appointment of cadres, to reduce the possibility of promoting those suspected of corruption and to further strengthen the functions of organization departments, organization departments at all levels have placed more emphasis on formative evaluation, and have carried out exploration and experiments about the usual assessment, based on the conclusive evaluation of regular assessment. The basic measure it has adopted is to record and evaluate the political morality and work process of cadres.

The usual assessment consists of political morality and work performance. The assessment of political morality consists of working attitude, moral character, work style, attendance, etc. The assessment of work performance focuses on recording and evaluating the completion of goals at different stages, daily tasks and tasks assigned by leaders, with stress on position responsibilities and work responsibilities. The assessment indicators consist of work schedule, periodical results, working quality, budget implementation, etc.

The procedures of the daily assessment consist of processes such as the personal records of work (record of completion of work within a specific period of days and months, form of usual assessment and self-evaluation), instant evaluation by superiors (leaders in charge of departments at a higher level evaluate cadres and adopt forms such as ranking and make comments to determine the results of the usual assessment based on the records of work and daily performance of these cadres) and aggregate results of assessment (regularly collect the results of the usual assessment, and supervise and check the quality of assessment by adopting methods such as compiling statistics, sampling and listening to the opinions of the general public).

The daily assessment is not only one of the ways to inspect the selection of cadres, but also an important basis for conclusive evaluation. The results of this assessment are generally used as an important reference for the selection and appointment of cadres. Besides the above mentioned daily assessment that centers around records of work, the daily assessment of leading cadres also includes individual discussions, investigation of specific items, inspection of the inspection team, audit of the economic responsibility of leading cadres, attending democratic meetings, debriefing reports on the work and morality of leading party cadres and annual work conference, which are all important measures for the usual assessment. While dealing with major events, the completion of major tasks and personal interests, the usual assessment focuses on assessing leading cadres' political attitude, sense of responsibility, ability to handle affairs and self-requirement, regularly carrying out public opinion polls, analysis of achievements, systematically collecting important statistics of economic and social development and opinions of evaluation provided by functional departments, strengthening daily accumulation and comprehensive analysis, so as to form a very rich body of materials of the usual assessment and provide a more objective and comprehensive reference for the selection and appointment of cadres.

Chapter 8

Discipline and Supervision of the Selection and Appointment of Cadres

In order to ensure a regulated operation of the selection and appointment of cadres and a timely detection and correction of any malpractices in this work, an effective regulation system has been developed. It includes work discipline that the personnel who select and who are to be selected should comply with in the process of selecting and appointing cadres, the work mechanism by which discipline inspection departments exercise supervision in the whole process of selecting and appointing cadres, and the regulations that are used for holding accountable those who commit fraud or have other problems in the selection and appointment of cadres. These regulations concerning discipline, supervision and accountability are very important components of the system of selecting and appointing cadres. Some appear in *Regulations on the Selection and Appointment of Leading Cadres of the Party and Government*, and some have been promulgated and implemented as separate documents by the party Central Committee or its organization and disciplinary inspection departments.

1 Discipline

(1) Connotation of discipline in the selection and appointment of cadres

Discipline usually refers to the norms of behavior that a social organization formulates for each of its members to abide by, in order to maintain its overall interests and guarantee its normal operation. These norms of behavior regulate organization members, what they can't do and what actions can't be adopted, and what responsibilities should be borne and what punishment to take in violation of these norms of behavior.

The discipline of the selection and appointment of cadres refers to mandatory and binding norms of behavior that party organizations have formulated for the purpose of maintaining their overall interests, ensuring the normal order of leading cadres of the party and the government, and guaranteeing the normal operation of the selection and appointment of cadres. Every leading cadre of the party and government should abide by these disciplines and receive punishment in case of violation, whether he is the one who selects or the one who is to be selected.

The discipline of the selection and appointment of cadres fully embodies the overall requirements and work norms by which the CPC run the party strictly and conduct strict supervision over its cadres. These disciplines are all targeted and operable.

(2) Discipline of the selection and appointment of cadres

The CPC has always attached great importance to the discipline of the selection and appointment of cadres. In December 2010, in order to ensure the smooth development of the fixed-term appointment system, the Commission for Discipline Inspection and the Central Organization Department proposed 'five strict prohibitions, 17 prohibitions and five dispositions', which systematically put forward very operable norms of behavior for the selection and appointment of cadres (especially fixed-term positions), with an emphasis on exercising strict discipline, maintaining the seriousness of the leadership transition and severely handling violations of discipline. The 'five strict prohibitions, 17 prohibitions and five dispositions' are:

First, strict prohibition on canvassing votes and practicing bribery in selection. No one is allowed to engage in non-organizational activities such as canvassing votes in a democratic recommendation, democratic evaluation, or organizational inspection and selection, and nor is he allowed to seek favor through arranging banquets, tours or other consumption activities, making phone calls, sending text messages, visiting voters, commissioning or inciting third parties to canvass votes, or organizing recreational activities; nor is he allowed to bribe other representatives or participate or assist in canvassing votes for others. Should anyone be caught engaging in canvassing votes for himself, he must be expelled from the list of candidates for inspection, or be ordered to resign, expelled, demoted or dismissed according to the law, or be punished according to the laws and rules; should anyone be caught engaging or assisting in canvassing votes for others, he must be punished in the same way as those who canvass votes for themselves.

Second, strict prohibition on buying and selling official titles. No one is allowed to bribe others for the purpose of seeking promotion, dispatch, transfer and retention of the post, or getting higher remuneration than the positional ranking; nor is he allowed to ask for, accept, or to ask for and receive bribes in a disguised form for the purpose of using his power to assist others in seeking promotion, dispatch, transfer and retention of a post, or receiving higher remuneration than the positional ranking; should anyone get caught buying and selling official titles, he must be suspended and dismissed, and then get punished and disciplined by the organization in line with the seriousness of the circumstances; should anyone be suspected of a crime, he must be transferred to judicial bodies according to the law; should any official title be obtained through bribery, it must be resolutely abolished.

Third, strict prohibition on craving an official position through unfair means. No one is allowed to use unfair means such as exploiting connections, securing advantages through influence or coercion to seek positions or a higher remuneration than the positional ranking; nor is he allowed to hand out official posts and make promises to grant special favors, or to intercede and solicit favor on behalf of others for their promotion or transfer. Should anyone get caught craving an official position through unfair means, he must be excluded from the promotion, and be subject to criticism and education and be disciplined by the organization in line with the seriousness of his acts, which must be recorded and filed in his personal files; should anyone get caught handing out official posts and making promises to grant special favor, or lobbying, interceding and soliciting favor on behalf of others for their craving an official position, he must be subject to harsh criticism, and be held accountable if his acts cause serious consequences such as a failure of personnel oversight or selecting and appointing an unsuitable person.

Fourth, strict prohibition on the illegal use of people. No one is allowed to violate the regulated procedures in the selection and appointment of cadres; nor is he allowed to engage in the surprise promotion and adjustment of cadres; nor is he allowed to practice cronyism and name certain cadres in promotion and adjustment; nor is he allowed to expand the number of leading cadres beyond the regulated number or seek a higher remuneration of positional ranking; nor is he allowed to take advantage of his official duties to interfere with the selection and appointment of his subordinates or in the places and departments where he used to work; nor is he allowed to disclose democratic recommendation, democratic evaluation, inspection deliberation or discussion about the choice of candidates. Should the determination of the appointment of cadres violate the regulations, it must be annulled and relevant people must be held accountable.

Fifth, strict prohibition on interfering with leadership transfer. No one is allowed to prevent representatives from exercising their rights to vote, to be selected and to vote for specific decisions by coercion or cheating; nor is he allowed to fabricate and spread rumors, or accuse, insult or slander others; nor is he allowed to give souvenirs as presents to representatives or disseminate promotional materials in the period of the leadership transfer; nor is he allowed to block an investigation or the handling of a violation of discipline during the period of leadership transition. Should anyone get caught disrupting or blocking a leadership transfer, he must be severely punished or transferred to the judicial bodies if suspect of a crime.

Drawing on 'five strict prohibitions, 17 prohibitions and 5 dispositions', *Regulations on the Selection and Appointment of Leading Cadres of the Party and Government* that was revised on January 14, 2014 further enriched work discipline for the selection and appointment of cadres, and put forward the disciplinary requirements of '10 prohibitions'. In the selection and appointment of cadres of the party and government, we should ensure that all the provisions in the regulations are strictly implemented and the discipline of '10 prohibitions' closely followed. Under these disciplines, no one is allowed to:

- over-staff leading positions, promote leading cadres beyond the authority of the institutions, set official titles without authorization or increase cadres' remuneration according to positional ranking;
- use unfair means to secure a position for oneself or another;
- recommend, inspect, deliberate, discuss or determine the appointment and dismissal of cadres;
- disclose information about the motion, democratic recommendation, democratic evaluation, inspection, deliberation, discussion or decision of the appointment and dismissal of cadres;
- conceal or distort the truth in the inspection of cadres;
- engage in activities such as canvassing votes in a democratic recommendation, democratic evaluation, inspection by the organization or selection;

- take advantage of his official duties to interfere with the selection and appointment of his subordinates, or do so in places and departments where he used to work;

- suddenly promote or adjust cadres during work transfer or institutional changes, without adopting normal procedures;

- hand out official posts or make promises, practice cronyism or engage in malpractices for selfish ends;

- alter a cadre's files, or falsify a cadre's status, age, length of service, party standing, educational background, experience, etc.

Mainly set up to address existing problems in the work of selection and appointment of cadres, these '10 prohibitions' have important binding forces for maintaining the authority and seriousness of the selection and appointment of cadres.

For example, according to relevant requirements (usually determined by commissions in charge of personnel establishments of the central and local governments) about the structure of the institutions and staff, the number and ranking of the positions (mainly refers to positional ranking) for leading cadres in each and every institution of the party and government are clearly defined, and the selection and appointment of cadres can only be carried out within the range of that number and positional ranking. Should anyone over-staff the leading positions, promote leading cadres beyond the authorization of the institutions, set up official titles (assistant, high counselor, adviser) without authorization or increase a cadre's remuneration according to positional ranking, he must be found to be violating the discipline.

Taking another example, a cadre's files are an important basis for the historical and comprehensive inspection and understanding of a cadre, embodying his credibility, reflecting the level of management of the organization (personnel) department. The authenticity of a cadre's files offers a basic guarantee of the seriousness of the cadre's work, and any attempt to alter, forge or falsify the cadre's files, important qualifications and records of service leads to a serious violation of law and discipline.

Should anyone get caught violating the discipline of selection and appointment, he must be subject to severe punishment by the organizations and discipline inspection agencies at all levels. Since the 18th CPC National Congress, the party Central Committee has attached great importance to investigating and handling violations of discipline, stressing the need to treat them seriously and to take a zero-tolerance approach. It needs to ensure that every attempt of violation is tracked down and handled immediately. The people concerned and those in charge will be made accountable, thus making the discipline of the organization a 'high-voltage power line'. To a certain extent, strict discipline serves as a lifeline for the selection and appointment of cadres.

Article 62 in *Regulations on The Selection and Appointment of Leading Cadres of the Party and Government* clearly stipulates that any action violating the discipline of the organization must be seriously investigated and, if necessary, punished. Should any violation of the regulations in selection and appointment occur, the chief and other relevant leaders of party committees (party group), relevant leaders and other directly responsible people of the organization and personnel departments would be held accountable. *Regulations on The Disciplinary Sanction of the CPC* implemented on January 1, 2016 makes a clear regulation on the disciplinary sanction in case of violation of the discipline of the selection and appointment of cadres.

Special column: Regulations on disciplinary sanction in case of violation of the discipline of the selection and appointment of cadres

Article 72 in *Regulations on the Disciplinary Sanction of the CPC* clearly stipulates that, should anyone get caught committing any of the following acts, he must be given a warning or serious warning; if the circumstances are relatively serious, he will be removed from the party post or placed on probation without losing his party post; if the circumstances are serious, he must be expelled from the party:

- engaging in canvassing votes for oneself or others and participating in other non-organization activities in the democratic recommendation, democratic evaluation, inspection by the organization and inner-party election;

- participating in non-organization activities, organizing, urging and prevailing on others in votes for election and decision-making, which violate the principles of the organization, in the law-regulated voting and electing activities;

- engaging in participating in other activities that violate the party constitution, party regulations and party rules in the election.

Article 73 in *Regulations on the Disciplinary Sanction of the CPC* clearly stipulates that, in the work of selecting and appointing cadres, the directly responsible people and relevant leaders in charge must be given a warning or a serious warning in case of disciplinary violations in the selection and appointment of cadres if the circumstances are relatively minor; they will be removed from their party posts or placed on probation without losing their party posts if the circumstances are relatively serious; they will be expelled from the party if the circumstances are serious.

Should negligence or mistakes be found relating to the selection and appointment of cadres and have caused serious consequences, the directly responsible people and relevant leaders in charge must be handled in accordance with the above-mentioned regulations.

2 Supervision on selection and appointment

The most striking feature of the selection and appointment of cadres in the CPC is a relative balance between adhering to the principle of placing cadres under the rule of the party and strengthening the supervision of cadres. In the actual operation and practice of selection and appointment, adhering to the principle of placing cadres under the rule of the party means that party committees at all levels are in charge of the recommendation, appointment and dismissal of cadres, wielding the power to guide and decide in the selection and appointment process. The corresponding institutional arrangement is to strengthen the supervision of cadres, which includes supervision over the cadres and party committees at all levels and their leading bodies. Of all the political parties in the world, the CPC implements the most powerful system and practice of supervision over the selection and appointment of its cadres.

(1) System of supervision and regulation

Article 62 in *Regulations on the Selection and Appointment of Leading Cadres of the Party and Government* clearly stipulates that supervision over the selection and appointment should be strengthened. Three other provisions in the regulations concern supervision over the selection and appointment of cadres, clearly defining the main body and methods for supervision.

Article 64: party committees (party groups) and their organization and personnel departments exercise supervision and inspection over the selection and appointment of cadres and over the implementation of this provision, handle accusations and appeals, prevent and correct acts in violation of this provision, and propose suggestions and opinions on how to handle the violation. Bodies of disciplinary inspection and supervision and inspection agencies are in charge of supervision and inspection over the selection and appointment of cadres in accordance with the relevant regulations.

Article 65: a joint conference system with the participation of organization and personnel departments, disciplinary inspection and supervision bodies, and other relevant departments is introduced to propose suggestions and opinions on communication, exchange of information, and supervision over selection and appointment. Organization and personnel departments are responsible for convening joint conferences.

Article 66: party committees (party groups) and their organization and personnel departments must strictly enforce this provision and consciously accept supervision from the organizations and the general public. Bodies at the lower level, party members and the general public have the right to accuse and appeal any violations of discipline and regulations to party committees (party groups) at the higher level and their organization and personnel departments, and bodies of disciplinary inspection and supervision, for the departments and agencies in charge to investigate and handle.

Party committees at all levels and their organization and personnel departments exercise supervision and inspection over the selection and appointment of cadres and over the implementation of provisions. Generally, special agencies are established for the supervision over and management of cadres within party committees and their organization departments at all levels to be responsible for handling accusations and appeals, stopping and correcting acts in violation of this provision, and proposing suggestions or opinions for handling by relevant responsible persons. At the same time, the party's disciplinary inspection bodies (and supervisory institutions for the supervision of non-party cadres) and inspection agencies also exercise inspection and supervision over the selection and appointment of cadres, and handle issues involved in violating the party's discipline and regulations.

(2) Measures and methods of supervision

Supervision and inspection of the selection and appointment of cadres has a multi-faceted, three-dimensional pattern. It involves a number of institutions and the use of various methods, forming a relatively effective supervisory mechanism.

1) Supervision by organization and personnel departments of party committees

Most problems found in the work of the selection and appointment of cadres have a direct bearing on the failure to strictly follow the relevant provisions in the selection and appointment of cadres. Therefore, party committees and organization and personnel departments should, above all, supervise their own territory, conduct regular supervision and inspection, take responsibility for handling accusations and appeals, prevent and correct acts in violation of this provision, and propose suggestions or opinions for the handling of relevant responsible people. Supervision and inspection comprise: whether the elected cadres meet the standards and requirements, whether the positions are over-staffed, how these elected cadres were recommended, whether the motion and deliberation were in accordance with the regulations, etc. Special attention should be paid to verify materials related to the appointment and dismissal of cadres, original materials about democratic recommendation, materials about the inspection of cadres, and conference records for discussion of cadres by party committees and party groups. It is also important to rely on the general public, and to listen to different views. When necessary, a questionnaire should be used in larger areas to solicit public views.

Since 2015, the Organization Department of the Central Committee of the CPC has begun to implement a series of strict investigations and verifications of cadres before their appointment, following the principle of 'reviewing the files of cadres when promotion is involved', 'verifying the relevant issues of an individual's report when promotion is involved', 'listening to the advice and opinions of disciplinary inspection and supervision bodies when promotion is involved', 'investigating well-grounded reports of petition letters relating to cadres under inspection when promotion is involved'. At the same time, the Organization Department of the Central Committee of the CPC also promulgated and implemented *A Number of Opinions on How to Strengthen Documentary Work in the Selection and Appointment of Cadres*, stipulating that backward tracking is undertaken for the selection and appointment of cadres when promoted cadres are suspected of corruption. These strict internal supervisory measures have played an important role in ensuring the quality of the selection and appointment of cadres.

Even when the heads of party committees that are responsible for the selection and appointment of cadres leave their present job, they also need to strictly inspect their duties performed in the selection and appointment of cadres before departure. In 2010, the Organization Department of the CPC Central Committee promulgated *Methods for the Inspection of the Duties of Party Secretaries at City or County Level Performed in the Selection and Appointment of Cadres before their Departure (Provisional)*. It stipulates that, when party secretaries at city or county level are about to leave due to reasons such as promotion, position transfer within the same rank or retirement, the organization departments of party committees at higher levels are responsible for inspecting their duties performed in the selection and appointment of cadres before their departure. This should cover implementation of the party line, principles and policies for cadres during their term of service; the selection and appointment of cadres for party committees at city or county level during their term of service; the nature of the selection and appointment of cadres in the area during their term of service; enforcement of discipline of organization and personnel during their term of service and especially information about whether there are sudden promotions and adjustments of cadres before their departure; information on the supervision and management of cadres' work during their term of service.

The means for inspection is to conduct a democratic review of the duties performed by departing party secretaries at city or county level in the selection and appointment of cadres during their term of service and cadres newly appointed by party committees at city or county level, to solicit opinions from cadres and the public through conducting individual interviews, holding seminars, issuing appeals and so on, and to review the material about the appointment and dismissal of cadres. The results serve as an important basis for the evaluation and appointment of party secretaries at city or county level. If the overall evaluation of their duties performed in the selection and appointment of cadres ranked as 'satisfactory' or 'basically satisfactory' fail to account for two thirds of the total rate, or if the overall evaluation of the environment for the appointment of cadres ranked as 'good' or 'relatively good' fail to account for two thirds of the total, organization departments will assess the relevant cadres, adopt measures to handle them, and block their promotion. If the democratic review of a newly appointed cadre is not satisfactory, party sectaries at city or county level should give an explanation.

2) Supervision by patrol inspection agencies

Supervision by patrol inspection agencies is an important systematic innovation of the CPC.

Chapter 8

The party Central Committee and commissions of provinces, autonomous regions and municipalities directly under the central government implement the patrol inspection system and have established specialized agencies to supervise patrol inspection over leading bodies and the other members of party organizations at lower levels. According to *Regulations on Patrol Inspections of the CPC (Provisional)*, patrol inspection agencies supervise leading bodies and the other members of party organizations in the following aspects: implementation of the party's line, principles, policies and resolutions, decisions, and, particularly, of Deng Xiaoping Theory, the important thought of 'Three Represents' and scientific outlook on development; the implementation of democratic centralism, the implementation of accountability for party conduct and government morality and the government's self-construction in building an honest and diligent government; the development of work style and the selection and appointment of cadres. Patrol inspection teams will focus their investigation and supervision work on whether there is malpractice or corruption, such as buying and selling official titles, canvassing votes and practicing bribery at an election, and promoting cadres in violation of regulations.

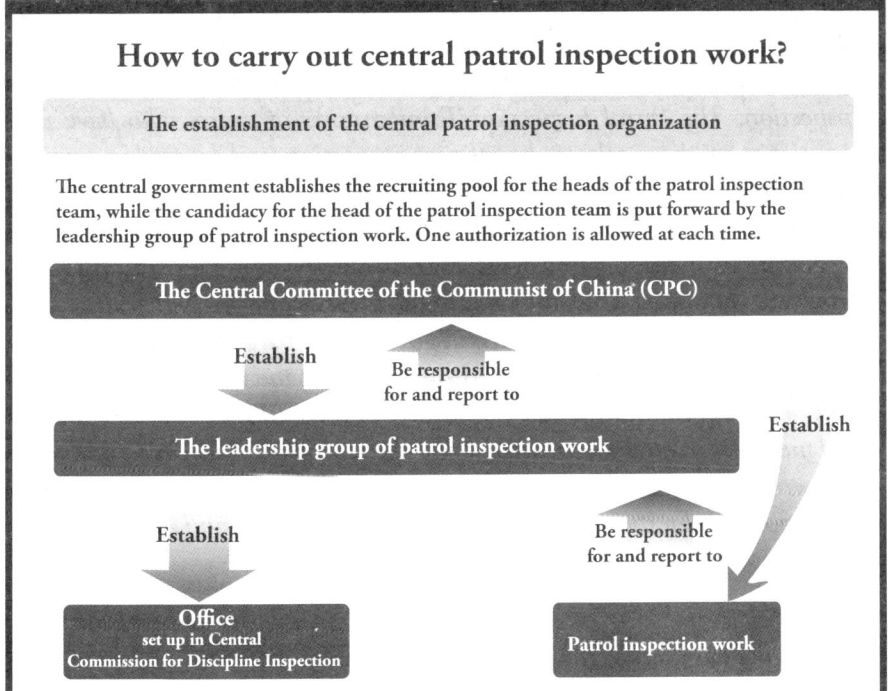

Table 8-1 Mechanism and constitution of the Central Patrol Agency
Source: *Qiushi*, October, 30, 2013

Special column: The patrol inspection system and agency

The patrol inspection system is a unique new system within the CPC and a strategic and institutional arrangement for the supervision of the party. It is the system by which the party Central Committee, Central Commission for Discipline Inspection and the provincial (provinces, autonomous regions, municipalities directly under the central government) party committees exercise supervision over leading bodies and the other members of party organizations at lower levels according to relevant regulations, through establishing specialized patrol inspection agencies. In 2003, The Central Committee of the CPC promulgated Regulations on Inner-Party Supervision of the CPC (Provisional), *making the patrol inspection system one of the most important systems of supervision in the form of inner-party laws. In July 2009, The Central Committee of the CPC issued* Regulations on Patrol Inspection of the CPC (Provisional), *making a systematic specification for the patrol inspection system.*

Patrol inspection agencies include the leadership group of patrol inspection established by the Central Committee of the CPC which in turn consist of the Office of Patrol Inspection and Patrol Inspection Team. The Office of Patrol Inspection is the agency that undertakes day-to-day operations, which is placed under the Central Commission for Disciplinary Inspection. The Patrol Inspection Team consists of cadres who have rich experience in the work of disciplinary inspection and leadership, mainly responsible for patrol inspection. The Central Inspection Team is responsible for the patrol inspection of leading bodies and other members of party organizations: 1. leading bodies and the other members of the commissions of provinces, autonomous regions and municipalities directly under the central government and their counterparts at government party organizations at the same level. 2. leading bodies of party organizations and other members of the NPC standing committee and Committee of the CPPCC; 3. leading bodies and members of other departments that the central committee requires to be inspected. The patrol inspection teams of local provincial party committees are responsible for the patrol inspection of leading bodies and other members of its subordinate party organizations at all levels.

Patrol inspection teams are mainly responsible for supervision over the implementation of the party's line, principles, policies, resolutions and regulations, and the discipline by leading bodies and other members of party organizations. Supervision over selection and appointment is another of the most important aspects of their work.

The supervision of patrol inspection involves activities such as being briefed on the work report done by party committees (party organizations) in which patrol inspection teams visit and receive special reports by other relevant departments; attending as non-voting delegates relevant meetings, meetings of democratic life and debriefings on reports on the work and morality of leading bodies of party organizations; handling letters, incoming calls and visits that reveal problems among leading bodies and the other members of party organizations where patrol inspection teams visit; convening seminars; holding individual discussions with the leading bodies of party organizations where patrol inspection teams visit and other cadres and people; reviewing and copying materials such as relevant documents, files and minutes of meetings; conducting democratic evaluation, questionnaires on leading bodies and other members of party organizations where patrol inspection teams visit; conducting visit research on subordinate institutions and departments and localities where patrol inspection teams visit, in proper ways.

3) Supervision by the Discipline Inspection Group

The Discipline Inspection Group is a special agency that is dispatched to subordinate party organizations and government departments to exercise direct supervision and inspection by the Central Committee of the CPC and Disciplinary Inspection Commission of local party committees.

The Disciplinary Inspection Group is mainly responsible for: the supervision and inspection over the implementation of the party's line, principles, policies and resolutions by the departments and their institutions where they are dispatched; the supervision and inspection over the observance of national laws and regulations and the enforcement of important decisions of the CPC Central Committee, State Council, provincial party committees and governments; the inspection over cases of disciplinary violation by party cadres within departments and major and complicated cases of disciplinary violation in their institutions, the investigation of violations of national laws, regulations, party discipline, government discipline and regulations and discipline for the selection and appointment of cadres; handling the exposure, prosecution and accusation concerning party organizations, party members and cadres under the inspection of departments and their institutions.

The Discipline Inspection Group is mainly divided into the 'Stationed Discipline Inspection Group' that is dispatched by the Commission of Disciplinary Inspection and the 'Internal Discipline Inspection Group' established within various departments. The Stationed Discipline Inspection

Group is authorized by the Commission of Disciplinary Inspection of the Central Committee of the CPC and directly led by the Central Commission of Disciplinary Inspection of the CPC; the Internal Disciplinary Inspection Group is established by the department where it exists. The setting mode for the stationed agency of the Commission of Disciplinary Inspection of the Central Committee of the CPC has always been 'point to point' and 'one to one', that is, a stationed agency is placed in departments. In some regions, a combined mode of 'separate station' and 'attribution setting' has been adopted; in departments where power is relatively concentrated, the funding is relatively adequate, and government morality is at high risk, the 'one to one' mode has been adopted, namely, setting up a separate Stationed Discipline Inspection Group; in some other institutions, a joint Stationed Disciplinary Inspection Group has been established, in which a single Disciplinary Inspection Group is responsible for the supervision and inspection of several institutions.

The Disciplinary Inspection Group and the Patrol Inspection Group have quite similar ways of working. The former adopts ways such as reviewing relevant files, listening to special reports, convening seminars and holding individual discussions to inspect, supervise and verify existing problems in the selection and appointment of cadres when it comes to accusations and appeals concerning party members. The difference is that the Disciplinary Inspection Group investigates and handles cases, investigates and collects evidence in accordance with the law, and metes out punishment to cadres according to internal party regulations, about any violations of discipline and law in the process of supervision and inspection.

4) Supervision of the joint conference system

Article 65 in *Regulations on the Selection and Appointment of Leading Cadres of the Party and Government* clearly stipulates that we should implement the joint conference system joined by organization and personnel departments, disciplinary inspection and supervision bodies and other related departments, and propose opinions and suggestions on strengthening the supervision, communication and exchange of information in the work of the selection and appointment of cadres. The joint conference, which is convened by organization and personnel departments, is an important supervisory measure in the selection and appointment of cadres.

The routine work of the selection and appointment of cadres is carried out by organization and personnel departments. Disciplinary inspection and supervision bodies are responsible for obtaining information about any violations of discipline and laws by cadres. Although the supervisory body of cadres within organization and personnel departments has gained some understanding of such violations (through daily supervision, cadres reports and other related issues), it is still necessary to establish a connection between selection and appointment and agencies of disciplinary inspection in the process of the selection and appointment of cadres, and especially when inspecting whether the person in question is qualified for the position or the official title.

The establishment of the joint conference system can promote a better and more comprehensive understanding of relevant information in the selection and appointment of cadres for communicating and doing a good job in supervising the selection and appointment of cadres from multi-levels, multi-channels and in an all-around way, so as to ensure an objective, correct and authentic understanding of information about the appointed person and those who appoint them. Participants in the joint conference system includes those from organization and personnel departments, disciplinary inspection and supervision departments, organization establishment management departments, human resources and social security departments, audit departments and petition departments. Key elements include conducting communication, exchanging information, proposing opinions and suggestions, and supervising work in the selection and appointment of cadres.

5) Supervision by party members and the public

Common party members and cadres can exercise supervision over the process of selecting and appointing candidates through many channels. In this regard, the CPC has some effective institutional arrangements to ensure that common party members and cadres exercise supervision over the work of the selection and appointment of cadres through normal channels.

(a) Publicity system before the appointment of cadres

Regulations on the Selection and Appointment of Leading Cadres of the Party and Government clearly stipulates that we should implement the publicity system of newly appointed leading cadres of the party and government. Specifically, after the decision of party committees (party groups) and before the issue of a letter of appointment, those who are promoted to leadership posts below bureau level must be subject to certain publicity unless they are promoted to some special positions (such as those involving national security or confidentiality) or have already been publicized in the period of inspection at the term of service. The publicity should be authentic and correct for the implementation of inspection. The publicity period should last no less than five working days.

The publicity system for newly appointed cadres reflects the democracy and transparency of the selection and appointment of cadres, and ensures that common party members and the public know about and can participate in decision-making in the selection and appointment of cadres; it also serves as an effective way to supervise the selection and appointment of cadres, which is helpful in minimizing oversights and mistakes.

Generally, the publicity material includes a newly appointed cadre's name, gender, party affiliation, birth date, current position, work resumes, and even work performance, and family property in some localities. Modes of publicity consist of an announcement to the public and announcement within institutions. Some important leadership positions need to be publicized through newspapers, television, radio and other media channels. The internal posts within party organizations and government institutions generally need to be publicized within departments, units and institutions, usually involving the issuing of a public announcement and notice, putting up a notice or publicizing them in the local area network.

(b) System of 'one report and two evaluations'

In addition to the supervision of the selection and appointment of cadres through the publicity of newly appointed cadres, the Organization Department of the CPC Central Committee also formulated *Methods for the Standing Committee of the Local Party Committees to Report at the Plenary Session of Local Party Committees on the Work in the Selection and Appointment of Cadres and Subject it to Evaluation (Provisional)* in 2010. It requires that the work in the selection and appointment of cadres should be reported to all party members and their opinions be heard. This is an important measure for the implementation of the spirit of the 17th CPC National Congress and the fourth plenary session of the 17th CPC Central Committee and the strengthening of the supervision in the whole process of the selection and appointment of cadres. Its significance lies in the combination of organizational and democratic supervision, the organic combination of supervision over the whole process of selection and appointment, and the supervision over the effect, combination of the supervision over the candidates in the selection and appointment, and the supervision over the process of selection and appointment. It is an important institutional measure for democratic supervision over the selection and appointment of cadres.

In accordance with the provisions of the *Methods*, local party committees (usually the standing committees) deliver work reports at the plenary session of local party committees every year, making a special report on the selection and appointment of cadres during the year, and subjecting this work in the selection and appointment of cadres and newly selected and appointed leading cadres to democratic evaluation. It is therefore known as 'one report and two evaluations'.

'One report and two evaluations' is generally carried out at the plenary session of the local party committees (enlarged) at the end of the year or the beginning of the following year, or in the annual summary or annual assessment of leading bodies and leading cadres. The participants of the democratic evaluation are mostly composed of all the members at the plenary session of the local party committees, leading bodies of the People's Congress and the Political Consultative Conferences and governments at the same level, members of the standing committee of the party's Commission of Disciplinary Inspection, leading members of work departments of the party and government and people's organizations, and chief leading members of the party and governments at a lower level.

The annual summary and annual assessment of leading bodies and leading cadres of the internal institutions of the party and government should also include a report on the work in the selection and appointment of cadres and are subject to evaluation by other party members and cadres. At this time, most participants of democratic evaluation are cadres or members of the institutions.

The contents of the report include the overall situation of the selection and appointment of cadres, the implementation of cadres' party line, principles and policies, innovative measures and methods for the selection and appointment of cadres, the establishment of a healthy mechanism for selection, appointment and inspection, the resolution of malpractices in the appointment of cadres, and the main problems and improvement measures in the selection and appointment. Participants of evaluation should anonymously complete the *Form of Democratic Evaluation of the Selection and Appointment of Cadres* and *Form of Democratic Evaluation of Newly Selected and Appointed Cadres*. Newly selected and appointed cadres comprise those leading cadres who have been selected and appointed in the past year.

Organization departments of party committees at the higher level will assess those who fare poorly in the democratic evaluation and provoke strong concern from the public, hold those responsible accountable and press them to make rectification; should any cadre be found to have fared poorly in the democratic evaluation and provoke very strong concern among other cadres and the public, the organization department of the party committee at the same level must make an explanation about his selection and appointment, and mete out corresponding admonishment and punishment.

The system of 'one report and two evaluations' functions as a 'regular physical examination', playing a positive role in detecting the existing problems and standardizing the selection and appointment of cadres. Some departments and work units that gained low levels of satisfaction have made a deep investigation into the outstanding issues in the selection and appointment of cadres and made earnest efforts to rectify them, and thereby improving the work in the selection and appointment of cadres; some newly promoted cadres that had a relatively poor degree of satisfaction have won recognition by continuous self-correction. At the same time, new situations and issues have occurred in the practice of the system of 'one report and two evaluations', calling for effective solutions.

6) Social supervision

Social supervision in the selection and appointment of cadres includes the following: taking concrete measures to inform the public of the policies and regulations for the selection and appointment of cadres; the procedures of the selection and appointment of cadres; the standard conditions for the appointment of cadres; the basic situation of selected cadres. The personal resumes and position description of cadres appointed by party committees or governments at the provincial level are generally publicized through the media.

Social supervision of the selection and appointment of cadres is also reflected in the right of common party members and the public to know about and supervise the selection and appointment of cadres. The public have the right to report to party committees (party groups) at the higher level and organization and personnel departments, bodies of disciplinary inspection (supervisory departments) regarding the violation of discipline and regulations in the selection and appointment of cadres. Party organizations at all levels also lay special stress on the use of supervision of public opinion and expose some typical cases that have been investigated and dealt with.

(3) Continue to increase efforts to supervise

The selection and appointment of cadres is a very important link in cadre work. Exploring ways of strengthening the inspection of cadres and supervision over the whole process of the selection and appointment of cadres and other work, establishing an effective restriction mechanism, forming a full-range, multi-level and strong supervision system and truly placing the power of selection and appointment under effective supervision are an important feature of the system of the selection and appointment of cadres in China. In January 2014, in order to match the revision and implementation of *Regulations on the Selection and Appointment of Leading Cadres of the Party and Government*, the central committee of the CPC issued *Opinions on Strengthening the Supervision of the Work of Selecting and Appointing Cadres* at the same time, stressing the need to continue to strengthen and intensify its efforts in supervising the selection and appointment of cadres.

Aimed at addressing some existing problems in the selection of cadres, the *Opinions* proposed five specific supervision measures.

First, it requires party organizations and their work departments at all levels to conscientiously implement *Regulations on the Selection and Appointment of Leading Cadres of the Party and Government*, and strictly follow the principle and regulations to select and appoint cadres. It is manifested in conducting work in strict accordance with the stipulated principles, standards, conditions, qualifications, procedures and discipline, ensuring that there must be regulations to abide by and which must be enforced strictly. It prohibits selecting and appointing cadres in violation of prescribed procedures, interfering in the appointment of cadres in subordinate departments or former work units, falsifying the files of cadres, letting out confidential information, suddenly promoting and adjusting cadres, handing out official posts and making promises to grant special favors, practicing cronyism, engaging in malpractices for selfish ends, craving an official position through unfair means, interceding and soliciting favor on behalf of others seeking an official position, engaging in non-organization activities such as canvassing votes, overstaffing, promoting cadres at a standard higher than the institutions are allowed to authorize or increasing the remuneration of cadre ranks in violation of regulations.

Second, it requires a strict check on the morality of candidates and a resolute guard against the promotion of cadres suspected of corruption. It requires the strict inspection of party conduct and the morality of candidates, and the opinions of disciplinary inspection and supervision bodies should be listened to carefully. Should any candidate be reported as having problems with corruption of other problems and hasn't been checked or is still under verification, his appointment must not be delivered to the party committee (party group) for them to discuss and make a decision; should any candidate be suspected of having problems that do not constitute a violation of discipline, his case must be strictly investigated. We should carefully review the report on the personal matters of candidates. We should verify them and not promote or appoint those who do not truthfully report or deliberately conceal the particulars. We should strictly verify the files of cadres. We should carefully check information such as identity, age, length of service, party standing, education and experience, and clarify any doubts. We should carefully investigate and verify the reported problems about newly appointed cadres during the publicity period and should not let them go through the formality of appointment without clarifying the doubts.

Third, we should severely investigate and deal with a violation of regulations in the work of selection and appointment and resolutely rectify any malpractices. No matter whether it is a collective position transfer or a routine selection and appointment of cadres, we assume 'zero tolerance' towards a violation of organizational and personnel discipline. No case should be left untouched, ensuring that those found guilty of malpractice do not receive benefits and are severely punished. Should anyone get caught craving an official position through unfair means, he must be excluded from the promotion or appointment, the matter should be recorded in his files, and the person subject to admonishment and criticism or disciplined by the organization depending on the seriousness of his acts. Should anyone get caught canvassing votes or practicing bribery in the election, he must be excluded from the list of candidates or disqualified for the candidacy, and be ordered to resign or be dismissed, demoted if he has already been promoted, and be made accountable according to the discipline and laws if he practiced bribery. Should anyone get caught buying or selling official titles, he must first be suspended or dismissed, and then his case handled by the bodies that enforce the regulations and laws. Should the appointment of cadres violate the regulations, it must be declared invalid and rectified in line with the cadre management authority. Should anyone get caught lobbying, interceding and soliciting favor on behalf of others or interfere personally with the selection and appointment of his subordinate, he must be resisted and subject to admonishment and criticism or disciplined by the organization depending on the seriousness of his acts. We should improve '12380' as a comprehensive platform for collating accusations, uphold and improve the setting-up system for supervision, and carefully check and seriously handle problems concerning the selection and appointment of cadres that the public report on. We should intensify efforts to brief and expose cases involving the violation of regulations in the appointment of cadres, making them a warning and deterrent for others.

Fourth, we should establish a reverse check mechanism to strengthen accountability in the selection and appointment of cadres. We should conscientiously implement the relevant provisions in *Methods for the Accountability in the Selection and Appointment of Leading Cadres of the Party and Government (Provisional)*. Should problems such as the 'promotion of cadres suspected of corruption', sudden promotion and exceptional promotion in violation of regulations occur, we must investigate the whole process of selection and promotion. Should acts of malpractice or dereliction of duty such as concealing the actual situation and violating the procedures occur, we must not only handle those responsible but also hold those in charge accountable, getting to the bottom of the situation. Should a continuous or major violation of organizational and personnel discipline arise, and inadequate accountability towards the violation of organizational and personnel discipline is involved, we must hold accountable the chief leaders of party committees (party groups) and those in charge in the organization and personnel departments and other relevant departments. We should establish the documentary system for the selection and appointment of cadres to provide a reference for investigation and accountability.

Fifth, we should intensify efforts to conduct supervision and inspection. By implementing *Regulations on the Appointment of Cadres* as the primary task, we should strengthen supervision and inspection in the selection and appointment of cadres, focus on checking whether the procedures comply with the regulations, whether the orientation is correct, whether the atmosphere is upright and just, and whether the result is fair. We should strengthen the inspection process, conducting targeted and intense inspection on the outstanding issues that cadres and the public report along with the departments and units that are frequently accused; we should further patrol inspection relating to the selection and appointment of cadres; we should carry out a wide inspection, conducting an overall inspection over all units that have the authority to appoint cadres at different levels and in different department every three to five years. We should stress the importance of supervision to prevent problems before they happen, strictly implement the system for the related issues in the selection and appointment. Should there be a failure to report an issue that must be reported, it must be made null and void. We should prevent issues such as exceptional promotion in violation of regulations, cronyism and illegal appointment in the name of competitive selection. We should strengthen inspection over the results, adhere to and improve the system such as 'one report, two evaluations' and inspections upon leaving office, and effectively regulate the selection and appointment of cadres.

Sixth, cadres of organizational work should adhere to justice and uprightness. Organizational and personnel departments at all levels should place supervision over the work of selecting and appointing cadres in prominent positions. Institutions of cadre supervision should be responsible for the implementation of supervision, and institutions of cadre work should exercise supervision in combination with self-responsibility. Cadre inspection groups should implement the system of 'one post, two responsibilities', giving consideration to the inspection and supervision of the atmosphere in appointment work. Cadres of organizational work should conscientiously build up their party character, stick to the principles, keep just and upright, be willing to take responsibility, act in strict accordance with the policy of the party and the rules, regulations and procedures of the organization, take the lead in maintaining the seriousness of cadre work, and resolutely resist and rectify malpractices in the appointment process. Should anyone get caught violating the discipline of organizational personnel, he must be removed from the team of cadres.

3 Accountability

Article 63 in *Regulations on the Appointment of Cadres* stipulates that we should implement a system of accountability for the work in the selection and appointment of leading cadres of the party and government. Should negligence or fault occur and cause serious consequence, malpractices prevail in the appointment of cadres within departments and regions, those acts that receive strong public concern and those that violate the discipline of organizational personnel and are not handled properly, the chief leading members and other leading members of party committees, leading members of organization and personnel departments and organs of disciplinary inspection and supervision and other direct responsible persons must be held accountable.

In 2010, the CPC central committee specially formulated *Measures for Accountability in the Selection and Appointment of Leading Cadres of the Party and Government (Provisional)*, requiring that we should persist in following the regulations, handling violations, assuming responsibility while enjoying the rights, tracking down any negligence of duties and classifying responsible persons into five categories: chief and other leading cadres of party committees (party groups), chief leading cadres and other personnel of organizational departments, persons in charge and other members of the cadre inspection group, leading cadres and other members of the bodies of disciplinary inspection and supervision and other leading cadres and members; for each category, we regulate the main circumstances of accountability according to the difference in duties and rights in the work of selecting and appointing cadres. There are 39 kinds of circumstances in total. These five major categories of objects of accountability and 39 kinds of circumstances of accountability are quite specific. For example, *Measures for the Accountability* stipulates that, in the work of selecting and appointing cadres, should any of the following circumstances occur, the chief leading members and the other leading cadres of party organizations must be held accountable:

- conducting designated promotion and adjustment of cadres in violation of the procedures and regulations for the appointment and dismissal of cadres;
- determining the appointment and dismissal of cadres through occasional proposals;
- convening a meeting of party committees (party groups) in violation of the regulations to discuss and determine the appointment and dismissal of cadres;
- determining the appointment and dismissal of cadres or change the determination of the appointment and dismissal of cadres made at the meeting of the party committee;
- conducting the sudden promotion and adjustment of cadres;
- overstaffing a position for leading cadres or raising the remuneration of a position in violation of the regulations;
- inciting, instigating, forcing organization and personnel departments to select and appoint cadres in violation of the regulations or blocking or checking the disciplinary inspection and supervision bodies and

organizational personnel departments to investigate and verify issues in the selection and appointment of cadres and handle them in accordance with the regulations;

- violating the regulations relating to the selection and appointment of cadres and causing negligence and fault in the appointment of cadres, which in turn lead to adverse consequences;

- failing to act upon prevailing malpractices that are of strong concern to the public in departments and localities, and failing to effectively handle violations of the discipline of organizational personnel.

The specific ways of accountability include criticism and education, letters of self-criticism, organizational sanction, disciplinary sanction and criminal punishment. *Measures for the Accountability* contains a very specific description about who should be held accountable and how to hold them accountable. It has made an important breakthrough in solving the thorny problems concerning responsibility identification, becoming a milestone in building the system of the selection and appointment of cadres.

Chapter Follow-up Questions and References

Questions:

Chapter 1

What are the main characteristics of the selection and appointment of cadres in China?

Chapter 2

What are the standards, qualifications and conditions for the selection and appointment of cadres?

Chapter 3

What are the main principles involved in the work in the selection and appointment of cadres?

Chapter 4

What procedures should apply in the selection and appointment of cadres?

Chapter 5

How is supervision and management strictly carried out in the selection and appointment of cadres in China?

Chapter 6

What techniques are commonly used in the examination and evaluation of cadres during selection?

Chapter 7

1. How is the evaluation of cadres' morality carried out in the selection of cadres?
2. What are the commonly used methods for assessment and evaluation in the selection and appointment of cadres?

Chapter 8

What are the strict supervision and disciplinary regulations in the work of selecting and appointing cadres in China?

Bibliography:

Bureau One of Cadres of the Organization Department of the CPC Central Committee. *A Study Guidance to 'Working Regulations for the Selection and Appointment of Party and Government Leading Cadres'*. Beijing: Party Construction Reading Press, 2014

Examination and Evaluation Center of Cadres of the Organization Department of the CPC Central Committee, eds. *Instruction Manual of the Examination and Evaluation of Public Selection and Competition of Cadres of Party and Administrative Leaders*. Beijing: Party Construction Reading Press, 2010

Zhao Hongjun ed., *Technical Manual of Competence Evaluation of Chinese Cadres*. Beijing: Xinhua Press, 2006

Zheng Richang ed., *Evaluation of the Qualifications of Cadres*. Shanghai: East China Normal University Press, 2007

The Organization Department of CPC Central Committee. *Textbook of the Organization Work of CPC*. Beijing: Party Construction Reading Press, 2006

Wang Yang. *Construction of Party Systems in the New Era*. Beijing: History of CPC Press, 2006

Yang Danna. *Investigation and Thoughts on the Reform of Cadre Selection and Appointment System*. Beijing: Academy of Central CPC Press, 2008

Research Office (Bureau of Policy and Regulation) of the Organization Department of the CPC Central Committee. *Questions and Answers Regarding the Deepening Reform of the Cadres' Personnel System*. Beijing: Party Construction Reading Press, 2003

Wu Hanfei. *Research on the System of Public Selection of Cadres in China*. Beijing: Chinse Social Sciences Press, 2002

Research Office (Bureau of Policy and Regulation) of the Organization Department of the CPC Central Committee, ed. *Research on the Reform of the Personnel System of Cadres*. Beijing: Party Construction Reading Press, 2011

Research Office (Bureau of Policy and Regulation) of the Organization Department of the CPC Central Committee, ed. *An Extensive Research on the Reform of the Selection and Appointment of Cadres with Chinese Characteristics*. Beijing: Party Construction Reading Press, 2011

Li Min. 'A Historical Investigation into the System of Cadre Selection and Appointment' in *The Journal of Chongqing Social Sciences*. 11, 2011

Liu Junsheng. *Summary of the Personnel System in China*. Beijing: Qinghua University Press, 2009

The Organization Department of the CPC. *Textbook on the Organization Work of the CPC Central Committee*. Beijing: Party Construction Reading Press, 2006

Chen Zhong, Bachelor of Engineering and Senior Engineer, is currently Director of the Human Resources Department, China Executive Leadership Academy, Pudong. He has served in the Shanghai Municipal Information Technology Committee, the Organization Department of the CPC Shanghai Municipal Committee. Having long been engaged in the implementation of informatization projects, human resource management, and organizational and personnel work, he has rich experience in the promotion of government informatization, management of informatization projects, and organizational and personnel work. Chen was a former review expert for the Shanghai Municipal Science and Technology Progress Award and Shanghai municipal informatization projects, and standing director at Shanghai Computer Society and Shanghai Software Industry Association.

Zhao Shiming, doctor of psychology and professor, is currently deputy director of the Teaching and Research Department and executive director of the Research Institute of Leadership in China of Executive Leadership Academy, Pudong. He is also a member of the Teaching Committee, Academic Committee and Professional Title Recommendation and Review Committee, and has long been engaged in research and teaching in psychological evaluation and personnel selection. He was formerly deputy director of the Human Resources Department and director of the Division of Personnel in China Executive Leadership Academy, Pudong.

Other people engaged in the writing and editing of this book include Ren Zhen, Weng Yanjuan and Yang Changyon.